Hurricane Katrina:

Devastation on the Gulf Coast

by Debra A. Miller

LUCENT BOOKS

An imprint of Thomson Gale, a part of The Thomson Corporation

THOMSON

™

GALE

Detroit • New York • San Francisco • San Diego • New Haven, Conn. • Waterville, Maine • London • Munich

For more information, contact
Lucent Books
27500 Drake Rd.
Farmington Hills, MI 48331-3535
Or you can visit our Internet site at http://www.gale.com

LIBRARY OF CONGRESS CATALOGING-IN-PUBLICATION DATA

Miller, Debra A.
 Hurricane Katrina : devastation on the Gulf Coast / by Debra A. Miller.
  p. cm. — (Overview series)
 Includes bibliographical references and index.
 ISBN 1-59018-936-1 (alk. paper)
 1. Hurricane Katrina, 2005—Juvenile literature. 2. Disaster victims—United States—Juvenile literature. 3. Rescue work—United States—Juvenile literature. I. Title. II. Series: Lucent overview series.
 QC945.M49 2006
 363.34'9220976—dc22
                                                                    2005030656

Printed in the United States of America

Contents

Introduction

The Worst Disaster in U.S. History

I N 2005 HURRICANE season arrived as it does every year in the southeast region of the United States that borders on the Gulf of Mexico. This year, however, a record twenty-six named storms formed in the Atlantic, including thirteen major hurricanes. One of these, the August giant called Katrina, wiped out a vast stretch of the gulf coastline of Louisiana, Mississippi, and Alabama. Katrina will go down in history for more than terrifying wind and rain damage, however: Just when many thought the storm had passed and the worst was over, Katrina's storm surge—powerful waves that build up under a hurricane—caused Louisiana's Lake Pontchartrain to flood, virtually destroying one of the most beloved and colorful of American cities, New Orleans. The combined effects of Katrina left almost twelve hundred people dead, more than a million people homeless and displaced, and property and economic losses that measured in tens of billions of dollars. President George W. Bush, speaking on August 31, two days after Katrina hit, described the catastrophe:

> The vast majority of New Orleans, Louisiana, is under water. Tens of thousands of homes and businesses are beyond repair. A lot of the Mississippi Gulf Coast has been completely destroyed. [The city of] Mobile [Alabama] is flooded. We are dealing with one of the worst natural disasters in our nation's history. . . . This recovery will take a long time. This recovery will take years.[1]

The immediate aftermath of the storm was agonizing not only for traumatized residents of the gulf region but also for millions across the country who witnessed a slow, confusing, and poorly coordinated rescue effort unfold on television. Many thousands of people, mostly poor African Americans, did not join the massive evacuation of New Orleans before the storm and were trapped in their homes, climbing into attics and onto roofs to escape the rising waters. Many struggled to reach designated shelters—the Louisiana Superdome and the New Orleans Convention Center—both before and after Katrina hit, but these storm-damaged landmarks soon became overcrowded and filthy, with little food or water, no electricity or air conditioning, and relentless heat and humidity. Television cameras captured people's misery, fear, and anger as they waited for rescue for hours and then days, and widespread compassion for the victims soon turned to outrage at what many viewed as an inept, inadequate government response to the disaster.

This August 29, 2005, satellite image shows Hurricane Katrina striking the Gulf Coast.

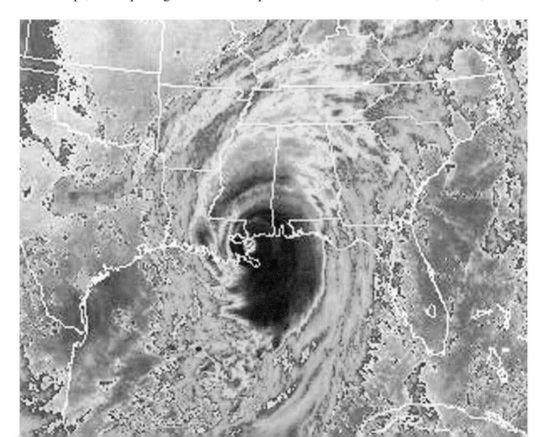

In the weeks that followed, stranded victims were evacuated from the disaster zone. Most had no homes or personal belongings to return to, and many suddenly faced the stressful prospect of finding new jobs, new schools, and new homes in unfamiliar places. Slowly the region and the nation at large began to regroup from the catastrophe and plan for the future. The epic task of rebuilding virtually an entire city and coastline, however, promised to be one of the biggest challenges the country has ever faced. Early estimates of the government's share of humanitarian aid and reconstruction costs were at least $200 billion, a huge sum given an already large federal budget deficit. Concerns also mounted about how to prevent corruption and waste in the relief and rebuilding process when so much money was at stake and there was so little time to review and approve contracts.

Exposing Chronic Vulnerability

Apart from the cost, debate over rebuilding focused on several chronic issues of urban planning in this historically vulnerable region. Experts agree that more hurricanes are inevitable, and some scientists predict that, based on changing weather patterns, hurricanes even more devastating than Katrina are in store. Americans must then struggle to answer crucial questions: How can the gulf coast be rebuilt to withstand such killer storms? Even if rebuilding is possible, is it wise? Many of the worst-hit parts of New Orleans, for example, lie below sea level, and some experts argue that it is futile to rebuild when catastrophic flooding is sure to recur. Deciding not to rebuild destroyed areas, however, would disproportionately affect poor and black neighborhoods and perhaps lead to charges of racial discrimination and government indifference to the nation's poor. Such a decision would also permanently change ways of life in New Orleans.

More debate centers on the engineering challenges of building an improved levee system to protect New Orleans from future devastation. Environmentalists, meanwhile, focus on the damage to the coastal environment and argue

that levee reconstruction alone is not the solution: Success-fully securing the region against future hurricanes, they say, means restoring fast-disappearing coastal wetlands that act as sponges to provide natural protection against storm surges and flooding farther inland.

In the aftermath of the hurricane, New Orleans was plagued by both flooding and fires.

The failures in the federal, state, and local governments' response to Katrina also raised cries for improving the nation's emergency response and disaster planning systems. Despite huge budget increases for homeland security and disaster preparedness following the September 11, 2001, terrorist attacks, the storm revealed major glitches in both national and local emergency preparation and relief programs. In particular, Katrina highlighted the need for better evacuation plans for the elderly, the sick, and other people without transportation or the wherewithal to reach safety on their own. If the nation could not handle a predicted and widely publicized natural disaster, many wondered, how could it effectively respond to a sudden terrorist strike on a major city?

Political fallout from Katrina, too, has been considerable. The unimpressive response of the Federal Emergency Management Agency (FEMA), the nation's main disaster relief agency, and what was viewed as Bush's own failure to take charge of the situation caused a significant drop in the president's approval ratings and threatened to hurt the Republican Party's chances in the 2006 congressional elections. State and local officials from the gulf region likewise received their share of criticism for a lack of disaster preparedness and poor management of local resources in Katrina's aftermath. Officials at all levels countered that a storm of Hurricane Katrina's magnitude simply overwhelmed the best defenses and rescue efforts that humans could offer.

These important issues will take years, if not decades, to resolve. In August and September 2005, however, Americans in Katrina's path were concerned not with long-term plans but with immediate, life-and-death issues—getting out of the hurricane's way, protecting loved ones, staying alive, and helping others in desperate need.

1

In the Path of a Monster

THE SOUTHERN COAST of the United States is well known for its natural beauty, rich musical and culinary heritage, and unique regional and cultural charm. This heavily populated region is also known for its geographical vulnerability: It lies directly in the path of hurricanes that form in the Atlantic Ocean and Caribbean Sea and blow to the west and north every year between June and November. The long Florida peninsula often bears the brunt of these tropical hurricanes, but every part of the gulf coast has experienced Mother Nature's fury at one time or another. On August 17, 1969, for example, the Mississippi and Louisiana coast was blasted by what has been called the worst storm ever to hit the mainland United States, Hurricane Camille. With winds of more than 200 miles (322km) per hour and a storm surge of over 20 feet (6m), Camille roared onto the gulf coast, causing substantial flooding and property damage and killing 143 people. An even more deadly and destructive storm, however, arrived in August 2005: the monster hurricane named Katrina.

Katrina Hits Florida

The early stages of Hurricane Katrina were typical of weather patterns that brew in the Atlantic during the hurricane season. At 5:00 P.M. Eastern Daylight Time (EDT) on Tuesday, August 23, 2005, the U.S. National Hurricane Center (NHC) issued a routine advisory statement noting the formation of a tropical depression in the atmosphere over the southeastern Bahamas. On Wednesday, August 24, at 11:00 A.M., the weather pattern was reclassified as a tropical storm and given the name Katrina. At this point the storm had sustained winds of about 50 miles (80km) per hour and posed no immediate threat. However, NHC forecasts showed the storm strengthening and heading toward southeastern Florida. The danger was clear by 5:00 P.M. Thursday, August 25, when the NHC classified Katrina as a slow-moving Category 1 hurricane, with sustained winds of 75 miles (121km) per hour extending about 15 miles (24 km) from the storm's center.

Two hours later Hurricane Katrina made landfall in a densely populated area of Florida between Hallandale Beach and North Miami Beach. Its 80-mile-per-hour (129km) winds and torrential rains were frightening. As Scott Resnick, a Florida resident who rode out the storm in Hallandale Beach, explained, "We had wind coming from

United States Gulf Coast

two directions. It sounded like a super wind tunnel."[2] The slow-moving storm crossed the peninsula Thursday night, weakening somewhat over land but still carrying hurricane-force winds of about 75 miles (121km) per hour and dumping up to 2 inches (5cm) of rain per hour, with most of the force hitting Miami-Dade County.

By Friday morning, August 26, the storm had turned toward the southwest and moved out over the Gulf of Mexico. The hurricane left behind in Florida at least fourteen people dead, more than a million people without electric power, and an estimated $1 to $2 billion in property damage. Yet Katrina was still a relatively small hurricane. The center, or eye, of the storm was only 10 miles (16km) across, and hurricane-force winds extended only about 15 miles (24km) from the center.

Katrina Grows in the Gulf

Satellite images and measurements recorded aboard hurricane-hunter aircraft, however, soon showed that Katrina was rapidly growing stronger, feeding on warmer-than-normal gulf water temperatures as high as 90°F (32°C). At 11:30 Friday morning, the NHC issued a special advisory indicating that Katrina was now a Category 2 hurricane with sustained winds near 100 miles (161km) per hour. The NHC also warned that Katrina was expected to intensify and could reach Category 4 strength within seventy-two hours. Most alarming was the news that the storm was headed straight for New Orleans, the largest city in Louisiana, with the probability of a direct hit on the city as high as 90 percent. Such a direct hit could be devastating to New Orleans because much of the city, particularly the newer parts, sat in a low-lying bowl of land below sea level.

The original city of New Orleans, founded by the French in 1718 between the Mississippi River and a large estuary called Lake Pontchartrain, was limited to a crescent of higher land surrounded by natural levees and bayou land, separated from the ocean by dense coastal swamps. These swamps collected silt brought down the Mississippi

How Hurricanes Form

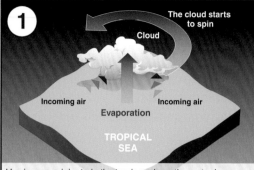

1

Cloud

The cloud starts to spin

Incoming air   Incoming air

Evaporation

TROPICAL SEA

Hurricanes originate in the tropics, where the water is warm and where the Coriolis effect is strong. Moisture rising from the tropical sea forms clouds. If winds are light, a mass of cloud can build up over one area. As the water vapor rises, the pressure falls and more air moves in. Under the influence of the Coriolis effect, the incoming air is deflected to the right and the cloud starts to spin counterclockwise.

2

Heat warms the air as water condenses

TROPICAL SEA

The moist air cools as it rises into the cloud, and the water condenses out as rain. This releases heat, which expands the surrounding air and the cloud itself. More air is sucked inward and upward in a continuous cycle. This is known as a tropical disturbance.

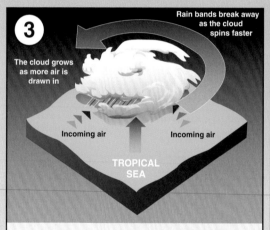

3

Rain bands break away as the cloud spins faster

The cloud grows as more air is drawn in

Incoming air   Incoming air

TROPICAL SEA

As the cloud becomes wider and deeper, the tropical disturbance becomes more organized and circular in shape.

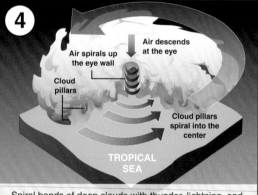

4

Air spirals up the eye wall

Air descends at the eye

Cloud pillars

Cloud pillars spiral into the center

TROPICAL SEA

Spiral bands of deep clouds with thunder, lightning, and heavy rain spin inside the tropical storm. At the center of the storm is the eye, a calm area around which everything rotates. As the rotating winds spin faster toward the eye, the Coriolis effect increases.

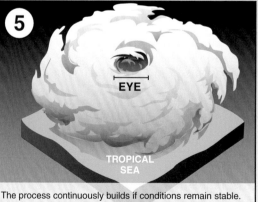

5

EYE

TROPICAL SEA

The process continuously builds if conditions remain stable. When sustained wind speeds reach 74 miles (119km) per hour, the tropical storm is officially designated as a hurricane. Typical hurricanes are about 300 miles (483km) wide with eyes between 12 and 37 miles (19–60km) across.

River, creating a soggy natural barrier that absorbed flood-waters and protected New Orleans from storm surges. In 1910, however, engineers drained the swamps with large pumps to create more dry land for new construction, greatly enlarging the city. Artificial levees (earthen or concrete walls) were built to protect the newly developed low areas, but engineers predicted that a strong hurricane could still submerge this region under several feet of floodwater. If the storm surge exceeded the ability of the pumps to remove water, or if the levees broke, this expanded part of the city could face major flooding.

Category 5

As predicted, over the weekend Katrina intensified over the warm gulf waters. At 5:00 A.M. on Saturday, August 27, Katrina was upgraded again, to Category 3, the level of a major hurricane. By midnight on Saturday, Katrina had grown even stronger, becoming a Category 4 storm with sustained winds of 145 miles (233km) per hour. Many gulf residents who had barely survived Hurricane Camille in 1969 began to think this storm could be just as dangerous.

By 6:00 A.M. on Sunday, August 28, Katrina had gone through yet another period of rapid intensification and was officially classified as a Category 5 storm, the highest level in the national hurricane rating system. At 9:00 A.M., storm watchers reported sustained winds of 175 miles (282km) per hour and wind gusts up to 215 miles (346km) per hour. The storm at this stage was massive as well as powerful, with hurricane-force winds extending 105 miles (169km) out from the center and tropical-force winds spreading as far as 230 miles (370km) outward. As Barry Keim, the Louisiana state climatologist, said, "That's when I realized we had a monster on our hands."[3]

An hour later the NHC called the storm a "potentially catastrophic hurricane"[4] that would bring dangerous winds and a high storm surge. Within minutes the New Orleans forecast office of the National Weather Service (NWS) issued an urgent hurricane warning for the southeastern and northern gulf coast, including the city of New Orleans. The

NWS warned that the storm was "a most powerful hurricane with unprecedented strength" that could cause "devastating damage . . . rivaling the intensity of Hurricane Camille of 1969." The NWS also bleakly predicted, "Most of the area will be uninhabitable for weeks, perhaps longer . . . the majority of industrial buildings will become nonfunctional . . . power outages will last for weeks . . . [and] water shortages will make human suffering incredible by modern standards."[5]

Officials Sound the Alarm

By this time government officials at all levels had been following Katrina's progress and issuing warnings to people in the storm's projected path for nearly two days. At 4:00 P.M. on Friday, August 26, after Katrina had crossed Florida and developed into a Category 3 storm, Louisiana governor Kathleen Blanco declared a state of emergency. Mississippi governor Haley Barbour issued a similar declaration for his state. On Saturday, at Blanco's request, President Bush declared a federal state of emergency in Louisiana, authorizing federal officials to release aid and coordinate disaster relief efforts. The crews of many off-coast oil-drilling platforms were quickly evacuated, and the platforms themselves battened down against the storm.

At 4:00 P.M. on Saturday, August 27, as it became clear that Katrina would indeed strike at or near New Orleans within thirty-six hours, Mayor Ray Nagin called for a voluntary evacuation of the city and said he was considering a mandatory evacuation. Nagin warned, "Ladies and gentlemen, this is not a test. This is the real deal. . . . Board up your homes, make sure you have enough medicine, make sure the car has enough gas. Do all things you normally do for a hurricane but treat this one differently because it is pointed towards New Orleans."[6]

On Sunday Bush extended the federal state of emergency to Mississippi and Alabama. That morning, less than twenty-four hours before Katrina's predicted landfall, Nagin issued a mandatory evacuation order for New Orleans —all residents and visitors were ordered to leave the city

The mandatory evacuation of New Orleans in advance of the hurricane produced an enormous traffic jam.

immediately. "We are facing a storm that most of us have long feared,"[7] the mayor said. Mandatory evacuation orders were issued, too, for other areas in southern Louisiana and for low-lying coastal regions of Mississippi and Alabama.

Existing disaster plans actually called for a minimum of two days to evacuate the gulf coast region. Now, with less than half that time left, both Louisiana and Mississippi officials took unprecedented measures: All lanes on interstate highways in affected areas were turned into northbound-only lanes to speed up the evacuation. Hundreds of thousands of gulf residents loaded their families and precious possessions into their cars and fled, jamming the area's gas stations and freeways in a fearful, frantic push to escape the storm. As New Orleans resident Linda Young explained while filling her gas tank at a city gas station, "I'm really scared. I've been through hurricanes, but this one scares me. I think everybody needs to get out."[8]

Some 150,000 people in New Orleans, however, were either unwilling or unable to leave. Many who remained did not own cars or simply had no money for bus or train tickets or airfare. In fact, some 100,000 people—about one-fifth of the city's population—lived below the poverty line, and large numbers of the poor stayed behind. Many who stayed were also elderly, ill, or had limited mobility. As seventy-four-year-old New Orleans resident Hattie Johns explained, "I know they're saying 'Get out of town,' but I don't have any way to get out. If you don't have no money, you can't go."[9] These stranded poor residents thus hunkered down, along with a few tourists and other stubborn residents, to ride out the storm. For those who could not, or would not, leave New Orleans, Nagin established two emergency shelters of last resort—the Louisiana Superdome, a massive, multipurpose sports stadium in the Central Business District, and the New Orleans Convention Center, a large meeting facility near the historic district known as the French Quarter.

Katrina Hits the Gulf States

Katrina blasted onto the gulf coastline at about 7:00 A.M. on Monday, August 29, as a slightly weakened but still strong Category 3 storm, carrying heavy rain and winds of over 127 miles (203km) per hour. Fortunately for New Orleans, the eye of the storm, surrounded by the fiercest winds, hit about 55 miles (88km) east of the city, sparing New Orleans a direct hit. Also fortunately, once over land Katrina's winds quickly slowed to about 100 miles (161km) per hour. The storm veered to the east at this point, moving out over water briefly. Many people in New Orleans breathed a collective sigh of relief as Katrina passed, believing the city had been spared the worst.

Nevertheless, Hurricane Katrina was strong enough to submerge entire neighborhoods along the Louisiana coast, hurl cars and boats everywhere, and rip apart trees, utility lines, signs, and buildings. Earthen levees were overwhelmed by the onslaught at several places, as storm surge direct from the gulf rose as much as ten feet (3m) above the levee walls and flooded about forty thousand homes in St. Bernard Parish (a political division similar to a county), east of New Orleans.

In addition, many high-rise buildings in the city itself had extensive wind damage. At the New Orleans Hyatt Regency, for example, most of the windows on the north side blew out and beds flew out of upper-story rooms. Roofing material on the steel-reinforced Superdome, where thousands of people had taken shelter, was stripped by the high wind, and the structure sprang significant leaks. The storm also knocked out electrical power throughout the region and forced the shutdown of oil refineries along the gulf coast.

Levee failures left nearly 80 percent of New Orleans under water. Flooded roads prevented emergency workers and aid from entering the city.

The Saffir-Simpson Hurricane Scale

Hurricanes are rated on a scale of Category 1 to 5 based on a system called the Saffir-Simpson Hurricane Scale. The ratings provide an estimate of a hurricane's intensity and are based mostly on wind speed.

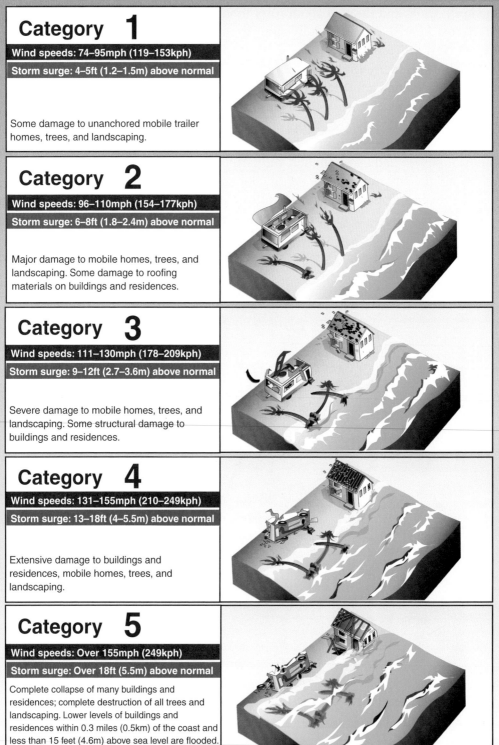

Category 1

Wind speeds: 74–95mph (119–153kph)

Storm surge: 4–5ft (1.2–1.5m) above normal

Some damage to unanchored mobile trailer homes, trees, and landscaping.

Category 2

Wind speeds: 96–110mph (154–177kph)

Storm surge: 6–8ft (1.8–2.4m) above normal

Major damage to mobile homes, trees, and landscaping. Some damage to roofing materials on buildings and residences.

Category 3

Wind speeds: 111–130mph (178–209kph)

Storm surge: 9–12ft (2.7–3.6m) above normal

Severe damage to mobile homes, trees, and landscaping. Some structural damage to buildings and residences.

Category 4

Wind speeds: 131–155mph (210–249kph)

Storm surge: 13–18ft (4–5.5m) above normal

Extensive damage to buildings and residences, mobile homes, trees, and landscaping.

Category 5

Wind speeds: Over 155mph (249kph)

Storm surge: Over 18ft (5.5m) above normal

Complete collapse of many buildings and residences; complete destruction of all trees and landscaping. Lower levels of buildings and residences within 0.3 miles (0.5km) of the coast and less than 15 feet (4.6m) above sea level are flooded.

Katrina soon made landfall again around 11:00 A.M. along coastal Mississippi and Alabama. Here, the storm's destructive force was even stronger than in Louisiana. Although it was still only a Category 3 storm by then, its 125-miles-per-hour (201kph) winds were still capable of pushing water from Mobile Bay into downtown Mobile, submerging large sections of the Alabama city. The hurricane also caused a record-high storm surge of 30 feet (9m) along the Mississippi coast, causing major flooding and damage in Mississippi's Harrison County. Early estimates reported at least one hundred of the county's residents were killed during the storm, and officials feared the toll would rise much higher. Governor Barbour toured the region and reported its near-complete destruction: "[The houses are] simply not there. . . . I can only imagine that this is what Hiroshima looked like 60 years ago."[10]

Hardest hit in Mississippi were the neighboring coastal towns of Gulfport and Biloxi. One Biloxi survivor, a navy veteran named Kevin Miller, clung to a tree and watched as people, some alive and some dead, were swept past him by floodwaters. He tearfully described his futile attempt to grab one desperate woman by her hair: "I just lost my grip."[11]

Biloxi was known for its gambling casinos, which had been built just offshore on floating foundations after local ordinances prohibited gambling facilities onshore. Katrina damaged or destroyed almost all of Biloxi's casinos, ripping entire structures from their moorings, sweeping them onto the shore, and depositing them on top of other crushed buildings. As Gulfport fire chief Pat Sullivan put it after visiting some of the areas struck by the hurricane, "Let me tell you something, folks. I've been out there. It's complete devastation. . . . What you're looking at is Camille II."[12]

All day Monday Katrina moved north across Mississippi. However, by the time the storm reached about 100 miles (160km) inland, around 10:00 P.M., it had weakened to tropical storm status. It continued northward through Tennessee, where it was again downgraded to a tropical depression. The storm that had been a monster only a day earlier then traveled farther north, bringing rain and winds to much of the northeastern United States, and all the way into Canada before dissipating. Weather experts would conclude, based on the extremely low pressure readings recorded at the storm's eye on Monday, that Katrina was the third strongest hurricane ever to hit the United States.

A Second Disaster in New Orleans

But as Katrina dwindled, the disaster was only beginning in New Orleans. On Monday afternoon the storm surge that followed the hurricane rolled into Lake Pontchartrain, north of the city, and breached the Seventeenth Street Canal levee, 2-foot-thick (0.6m) concrete flood walls lining the shipping canal that connected the lake and the Mississippi River south of the city. The canal flood walls, ranging from 17.5 to 23 feet (5 to 7m) in height, and a massive system of pumps were what kept many low-lying areas dry. Now the breaks in the flood walls allowed a second, slower flow of water from Lake Ponchartrain to flood the city.

New Orleans structural and civil engineers initially suspected that the cause of the flooding was overtopping—that is, water that rose higher than the walls and flowed over them, as the surge had flowed over earthen levees earlier in the day. Hurricane experts had warned officials days earlier that overtopping was likely. Mark Levitan, the director of the Louisiana State University Hurricane Center, had briefed Louisiana officials on Saturday, August 27, to expect 11- to 12-foot (3.4 to 3.7m) surges in Lake Pontchartrain. The briefing map also contained a message in red: "Levee overtopping predicted for west New Orleans but may also occur in New Orleans East and St. Bernard Parish."[13] The next day, the NHC issued a similar warning, suggesting that "some levees in the greater New Orleans area could be overtopped,"[14] and predicting storm surges up to 28 feet (9m) in the Gulf of Mexico and 18 to 25 feet (5.5 to 7.6m) inland.

After analysis of the flooding and levee breaks, however, engineers would conclude that the actual surge in the city itself was not higher than the 17.5-foot (5m) canal flood walls; rather, the walls broke because the soils at the foundations shifted and gave way. Emergency crews tried to drop huge sandbags into the breaches by helicopter to stop the flow before it inundated New Orleans, but the bags could not hold against the force of the water. In addition, many of the massive pumps normally used to drain storm waters from low-lying streets were themselves flooded, overheated, or without power (or operators, who had been evacuated), so they were useless against the rising waters.

By the end of the day on Tuesday, August 30, more than 80 percent of the city was underwater, as was most of St. Bernard Parish to the east. In Jefferson Parish, a heavily populated suburb west of downtown, floodwaters devastated thousands of homes. Most of the flooding occurred in

Major flooding throughout low-income suburbs like Saint Bernard Parish killed hundreds of residents and devastated several thousand homes.

Two people are rescued from the roof of their flooded New Orleans home on August 29, 2005.

largely residential, low-income areas that were from 6 to 20 feet (1.8 to 6m) below sea level. The worst-hit area was a section of east New Orleans called the Ninth Ward. Aerial photographs of these areas revealed block after block of structures flooded to the rooftops. In contrast, older parts of the city built on higher ground survived the disaster with limited flooding and damage. The most famous of these fortunate areas was the French Quarter, the city's premier tourist district, which contains numerous historic and architectural landmarks. Other areas that largely escaped serious damage were the Central Business District, the prestigious Garden and Uptown Districts (the site of Tulane University), and a residential area known as Algiers, located across the Mississippi River from the French Quarter.

For those grateful to have survived Hurricane Katrina's winds and torrential rains, the rapidly rising waters were a second, even more dangerous threat in New Orleans. In some places, the water was 20 to 25 feet (6 to 7.6m) deep within a few hours. Before long, miles of houses were almost completely submerged, and many people were forced into their attics or onto their rooftops to avoid drowning. One frantic city resident, Chris Robinson, was able to make a phone call from his home in east New Orleans. He pleaded, "I'm not doing too good right now. . . . The water's rising pretty fast. I got a hammer and an ax and a crowbar, but I'm holding off on breaking through the roof until the last minute. Tell someone to come get me please. I want to live."[15]

Thousands of residents were forced completely out of their homes; soon TV cameras captured images of groups of stranded citizens wading, swimming, or floating on makeshift rafts through floodwaters, looking for shelter. Tens of thousands headed for the Superdome, swelling its population to the breaking point. When the streets around the Superdome were themselves flooded, many thousands more struggled through the waters to reach the convention center, on slightly higher land about eight blocks away, creating another mass of bedraggled evacuees. At least three hundred people just waited for help on high ground, camping out in the hot summer sun on the shoulders of an elevated section of Interstate 10, the city's main freeway.

Many residents failed to reach safety; numerous bodies were reported floating in the city's floodwaters. Nagin said, "We know there is a significant number of dead bodies in the water. . . . Minimum, hundreds. Most likely, thousands."[16]

New Orleans Paralyzed

Aside from the human toll, the storm and flooding paralyzed New Orleans. On Monday, the storm knocked out all electricity throughout the city. In an interview that morning, Nagin described the city as completely dark with no clear way in or out. Most communications networks were also destroyed or inoperable, as cell phone towers, power stations, and telephone poles were knocked out by wind and water. Local television and radio transmissions, too, were disrupted. In some cases, government officials had to ask reporters to brief them on flooding and evacuee conditions, because the officials were not getting information any other way. A rare exception was the city's major daily newspaper, the *Times-Picayune:* Most employees were forced to move to a temporary base in Baton Rouge when a break in the Seventeenth Street Canal flooded its offices, but the paper managed to publish throughout the disaster.

Normal transportation into and out of the area also became almost impossible in the hours and days after the storm and the flooding. New Orleans's two airports were both underwater, major bridges were destroyed, and highways and surface streets became impassable. Transportation was largely limited to boats and helicopters, both of which were in short supply right after the storm. In addition, almost all of the city's businesses and industries shut down.

By Tuesday New Orleans was largely uninhabitable and almost completely isolated from the outside world. Coastal regions of neighboring Mississippi and Alabama were suffering as well and in dire need of help, but their plight was in some ways overshadowed by the tragedy unfolding in Louisiana. The Katrina disaster had just begun.

2

The Human Tragedy: No Shelter from the Storm

THE DOUBLE DISASTER of Hurricane Katrina and the New Orleans levee breaks produced a catastrophe unlike any the United States has ever experienced. Only a few times in U.S. history—the great 1871 Chicago fire, the 1889 Johnstown flood, and the 1906 San Francisco earthquake—have natural forces almost completely destroyed an American city. The disaster in New Orleans had a new dimension: Pleas for help from the thousands of people trapped in the flooded city without food, water, shelter, or other vital necessities reached the outside world by cell phone and televised images, but day after day, help failed to reach the victims.

A City Underwater

By Tuesday, August 30, much of the city of New Orleans was underwater and at least one hundred thousand people were stranded, including thirty thousand in the Superdome, twenty-five thousand at the convention center, and many thousands more still struggling to stay above water in the attics and on the roofs of their flooded homes. Governor Blanco ordered that everyone left in the city must be evacuated, and search-and-rescue efforts began. Rescue work, however, was slow and initially haphazard, as a small number of helicopters and boats picked people off rooftops one by one.

The skies had cleared, but in the searing late August heat and humidity, the urgent need for rescue soon became clear. Water mains had broken, making clean drinking water unavailable, and most fresh food supplies were contaminated by the flooding or soon spoiled without refrigeration. Power and communication outages were expected to last for many weeks and perhaps longer. Without air conditioning, temperatures inside many buildings topped 110°F (43°C), and people exposed to the heat and humidity outdoors were just as miserable as people indoors. And as far as the eye could see there was water, not clear but brown and smelly, contaminated by raw sewage, gasoline, and toxic chemicals.

After suffering through dangerous conditions in the Superdome, evacuees had to wait in long lines for transportation out of the city.

Most of the tens of thousands of stranded residents could do little but wait for news and help in the brutal Louisiana heat. Mothers' desperation grew as their vulnerable infants and young children became dehydrated, and pregnant women prayed not to go into labor until they were rescued. The sick, disabled, and elderly were stuck

without access to medications or medical care and began to die in the wretched conditions. As Blanco put it, "The situation is . . . just heartbreaking."[17]

Hellish Conditions in the Shelters

Ironically, some of the worst conditions developed at the sites designated as official shelters. As more and more people arrived, these holding pens soon became more like overcrowded prisons than safe havens.

On Tuesday the air conditioning failed at the drenched Superdome, turning the huge arena into a giant greenhouse, trapping the heat and humidity and baking those inside. The Superdome had been equipped before the storm with enough water and food rations to supply fifteen thousand people for three days, but these stores were quickly exhausted as twice that number of people came there for shelter. Next, the electricity went out. At first a few lights remained on, powered by an emergency generator, but the generator too soon stopped working, leaving people inside in complete darkness.

Things got worse: On Wednesday, August 31, the plumbing system failed. Faucets went dry, and toilets soon overflowed with human waste. The stench inside the Superdome was overpowering. On top of these horrors, gunshots were heard and rumors of rapes and murders spread among the crowds. Yet there was nowhere to run and nothing to do, except wait to be evacuated by buses that each day failed to arrive.

Similar conditions developed at the convention center, where refugees were directed because of overcrowding inside and flooding outside the Superdome. Here, too, there was no food, no water, and no electricity. Piles of trash and pools of urine spread, as did wild rumors of gunshots and violence. Stranded flood survivor Raymond Cooper, in a cell phone call to CNN news offices from the convention center, reported, "They have quite a few people running around here with guns. . . . You got these young teenage boys running around up here raping these girls."[18]

The credibility of these rumors increased when reporters who went to the convention center on Thursday, September 1, described numerous corpses lying unattended. As CNN reporter Chris Lawrence explained, "There are multiple people dying at the convention center. . . . There was an old woman, dead in a wheelchair with a blanket draped over her, pushed up against a wall. Horrible, horrible conditions. We saw a man who went into a seizure, literally dying right in front of us."[19] In fact, many of the rumors of violence were found to be untrue, but six people did die at the Superdome and four died at the convention center—

Frustrated by the lack of public transportation, some evacuees walked from the Superdome in search of assistance.

most from natural causes and preexisting illnesses, one of a drug overdose, and one an apparent suicide.

During the ordeal, television cameras captured image after image of desperate people begging for help. The Reverend Isaac Clark implored, "We are out here like pure animals."[20] Across the nation and around the world, people watched the TV news coverage of stranded disaster victims with growing outrage, aghast that such horrific conditions existed in one of the world's wealthiest countries. In addition, most of the stranded victims shown on TV were poor and black, revealing the harsh reality of poverty and racial divisions in the South. As *Newsweek* reporter Julia Reed explained, "The images of the thousands of African-American victims trapped by the flooding—there were some white faces, but not many—illuminated the city's stark racial and economic extremes. . . . [Many] were too poor, too sick or too old to join the exodus in time."[21]

Trapped in Flooded Buildings

Many other hurricane and flood survivors endured equally harrowing conditions, trapped in flooded houses and buildings as they, too, waited for help. The Web site of the *Times-Picayune* posted numerous calls for help from victims who managed to get word to friends and relatives. Resident Quan Vo, for example, reported that three hundred people were stranded in sewage-fouled water up to their necks at a Vietnamese church in New Orleans. He explained, "Many of the people are growing weak and sick from lack of food and water plus the heat. Some of them feel like they probably won't make it for the next day."[22]

Yet another wrenching Internet posting came from Jason Newton, who after the storm had received text messages by cell phone from his girlfriend, an obstetrics-gynecology resident at New Orleans's University Hospital. According to Newton's girlfriend, thirteen hundred people were stranded at the hospital without electricity, water, and food, and many patients were dying. On Wednesday, August 31, her message read, "No [news.] Water dropping. Gunshots and riot. Not safe."[23]

Countless distress calls came from family members outside the New Orleans region who were sick with worry about stranded relatives and desperate for their rescue. Daniel Melancon of Atlanta, Georgia, for example, pleaded for help for his sister, Denise, his great-aunt Orelia, and three small children who were trapped in New Orleans: "[They] are stranded on Veterans Memorial Blvd. where they were dropped off with NO FOOD OR WATER, they have been there for 3 days. . . . WHERE IS THE NATIONAL GUARD with food drop offs!!! THESE PEOPLE ARE ELDERLY and are in need of some sustenance!!! PLEASE HELP THEM."[24]

A few stranded citizens managed to contact the *Times-Picayune* directly. One cell phone e-mail message came from Robert James Ratcliff, who wrote that he was stuck in Algiers since Hurricane Katrina hit. Ratcliff pleaded:

> There are people over here dying, killing, robbing, raping. . . . This [is] my last resort. I have no other options. NO FOOD, NO WATER, NO ELECTRICITY. My two sons and I are doing our best to survive. . . . I have been trying to call numbers for help [but] I can not get through to any. I am able to communicate with family through the phone but they can't get in to get me out. . . . PLEASE, PLEASE, PLEASE, HELP ME GET OUT OF HERE!!!! I'M DESPERATE!!"[25]

The beleaguered New Orleans Police Department was deluged with telephone calls from all directions. Neliska Calloway, one 911 dispatcher, worked for forty-eight hours straight after the storm hit, taking countless calls from frightened citizens. She remembers one desperate call from a woman who had fled to her attic with the waters still rising. The woman was in labor with twins, begging for help. Later, emergency workers reportedly rescued the woman, but by then one of her unborn twins had died.

Looting and Chaos

As days passed without rescue, desperation turned to anger. Deep frustration led some New Orleans residents to break into closed stores, starting a citywide wave of crime

and looting. Most people took only what they needed for basic survival—food, water, hygiene or medical supplies. Some looters, however, were seen and filmed stealing televisions, jewelry, alcohol, and other nonessential goods, and a few stole guns and ammunition. Reports of violent armed robberies fueled rumors that law and order were crumbling.

Looting became widespread throughout New Orleans in the chaotic first days after Katrina struck.

By Thursday the situation in New Orleans was chaotic. Shots were fired at helicopters and rescue crews as they approached stranded people, forcing them to turn away for their own safety. Michael Brown, the director of the Federal Emergency Management Agency (FEMA), described conditions on the ground as "urban warfare,"[26] and FEMA officials reportedly ordered some boat rescue teams to halt their rescue efforts because of security concerns. Nagin finally was forced to order New Orleans police officers involved in the rescue effort to stop that important task and turn their attention to the escalating looting.

Surviving the Waters

As refugees began to make their way out of New Orleans's flooded areas, many told riveting stories of how they escaped death in the rising waters. Eighty-year-old Dorothy

Bates, for example, said, pointing to her chin, "I was flooded up to here. . . . I was standing on a ladder, trying to stretch my body. I knocked on my wall and shouted to my neighbor, 'Come and get me before I drown!'"[27] Bates was safely transferred to a shelter, where she waited until she could travel to Boston, to live with her son.

What Robert Newman Jr., a resident of hard-hit St. Bernard Parish, remembered most about the aftermath of the storm was the screaming. As rescue helicopters flew back and forth over the flooded neighborhood, he explained, "People [were] just screaming and screaming on every roof."[28] Eventually, Newman and his brother found a boat, which they used to rescue themselves as well as others. One of their successful rescues was an elderly couple who were found neck deep in snake-infested waters.

Sharon Billiot told a similar story of survival and helping others. She and her family survived the start of the hurricane at home but were soon threatened by flooding. They then escaped in a boat, which they paddled to a nearby church. Along the way, they encountered other victims of the storm. As Billiot explained, "We saw a man screaming from a telephone pole, but we couldn't reach him. . . . We were able to get another man off a roof though."[29] Eventually, they were airlifted out by helicopter.

Lucky but Still Suffering

Although the people lucky enough to escape New Orleans before the storm did not themselves face physical danger, many endured another kind of hell as they helplessly watched the disaster unfold from hotel rooms, shelters, and the homes of families and friends. New Orleans native Jackie Washington Skidmore, for example, fled with nine family members to a Marriott hotel as the storm approached. There, they watched in horror as television reports showed their homes completely underwater. They faced the future with all their possessions destroyed, no income, dwindling cash, and credit cards their only remaining source of funds. As Skidmore's son-in-law explained, "We thought we would be gone for three or four

Yearning for Ice

In the immediate aftermath of Hurricane Katrina, one of the most sought-after commodities, along with drinking water and food, was ice. As temperatures soared to more than 90°F (32°C) outside and often to well over 100°F (38°C) inside crowded buildings without electricity or air conditioning, ice was considered a necessity, not a luxury. Yet ice was almost impossible to find during this period. Most commercial supplies had been bought out before the storm by people hoping to keep their refrigerated food cold until the power came back on. The ice that was left after the storm was either stolen by looters or taken by authorities involved in the rescue work. A week after the storm, ice-filled tractor trailer trucks finally began pouring into the gulf region, and residents who could get to distribution sites said the occasion felt like Christmas. Suddenly, with just a little bit of ice, people's moods lifted, replacing depression and anger, at least temporarily, by smiles and laughter.

A National Guardsman takes a break from distributing ice to Katrina survivors. The lack of refrigeration or air conditioning made ice highly valued.

days. . . . Now we don't know when we'll be able to get back . . . if ever."[30]

Indeed, even the most fortunate of the evacuated city residents suffered great anxiety. One woman, described only as Patricia, safe in Texas with her family and blessed by news that her house had survived the disaster, expressed her worry in an Internet blog about the storm's effect on her business and finances. She explained, "We have been told that we will be able to return home in the next few days. With the joy of this news comes fresh anxiety—we fear what we will find, and the amount of work to be done is staggering. So we are all beginning to have sleepless nights again. . . . We don't know the state of our businesses. There is a tremendous amount of uncertainty."[31]

The future was just as uncertain even for business owners whose businesses were spared. David Carrington Sr., for example, learned that his house had been destroyed but his seafood company, Carrington Foods, made it through Katrina nearly intact. Thanks to a functioning generator, even his valuable inventory of perishable seafood was saved. But important links in his business chain were bro-

The business district of New Orleans remained flooded more than a week after the hurricane hit the city.

ken: The storm destroyed many of his shrimp and crab suppliers as well as the restaurants that bought his goods. Carrington hoped to stay in business, but without customers he did not know how long he could continue to pay employees, some of whom also lost their homes and possessions in the storm.

Searching for News of the Missing

With communications networks across the gulf coast severely damaged, the search for news from friends and family members missing in the disaster zone turned desperate. Countless informal information sites appeared on the Internet, full of posts pleading for word about a loved one or help for the stranded. Darrian Williams, for example, wrote, "My 81-year-old grandfather did not evacuate for the storm. He lives alone and has only one leg [and is] in a wheelchair. He's an insulin-dependent diabetic and may be out of insulin. Please help rescue my grandfather."[32]

Some of the most poignant pleas were those of distraught parents who had been separated from their young children during the storm or flooding. The plight of Lisa Moore and Larry Morgan and their ten children was all too common. Hurricane Katrina's storm surge sent waves of water through their New Orleans home. The family fled rising floodwaters into the attic, where for three broiling days they struggled to survive on a couple of cans of fruit cocktail, allocating just a few drops of juice per day to each of the younger children. Moore and Morgan took turns climbing onto the roof to wave a towel at passing helicopters, signaling for help. Finally, on Wednesday, August 31, a rescue helicopter hovered above the house and the couple was faced with a terrible dilemma: The helicopter could fit only five additional people, so Moore and Morgan had to decide which five of their children should be rescued. The desperate parents handed over the youngest four—ages two, five, ten, and eleven—who were growing weak from dehydration, and then thirteen-year-old O'Neil, who was instructed by his father, "Look after one another."[33]

The Moore children were taken to a Louisiana shelter, where O'Neil dutifully took care of his younger siblings. The remaining seven family members were eventually evacuated to a shelter in Austin, Texas, where they began a frantic search for the younger children. After many agonizing days, the five youngsters were located with the help of an Internet database. On September 15, coincidentally Larry Morgan's birthday, volunteer pilots flew the children to Austin, and the family was finally reunited.

In various forms this story was repeated again and again during the days after New Orleans flooded. The National Center for Missing and Exploited Children in Virginia received reports of forty-five hundred children missing or

Death and Destruction in Mississippi

Tony and Diane Brugger, co-owners and hosts of the historic Harbour Oaks Inn in Pass Christian, decided to ride out Hurricane Katrina. As Diane Brugger wrote later, they could not imagine the struggle and tragic loss they would face.

The night before the storm, we had the house clean, ready, & well supplied to take care of any evacuees the police might bring to us. Darlene (our housekeeper) and I had been preparing food all day and throughout the night we were feeding the EMTs and police. As we were 33 ft. [10m] above sea-level and [1969's Hurricane] Camille never made it into the house, we arrogantly believed we were safe. We took a brief nap at 3 A.M. Katrina had been taken down to a CAT 3. We were up at 5 A.M. and from 5–9:30 A.M. it went from bad to unbelievable. There were tornadoes and all of our plywood over the doors and windows were ripped off or blown out. We were in a 2nd floor bedroom . . . [when] the surge came. . . . The house started breaking up into 4 or 5 pieces. Both houses on either side were already gone. We were attempting to get to the billiard room to step out into the water when our apartment broke from the main house. We were in Tony's workroom at the top landing of the back stairs when the ceiling collapsed. Tony was caught in the corner and was taken down under the water.

Diane Brugger, Harbour Oaks Inn Web site, Bed and Breakfast Online, October 4, 2005. www.bbonline.com/ms/harbouroaks/.

looking for parents immediately after the storm. Gradually, this number fell as reunions were reported, but not all stories had happy endings. Though it is likely that many names remained on the list simply because families' reunions were not reported to the center, as of October 11 some 2,150 children across five states were still officially listed as missing or separated from their families.

Suffering in Mississippi and Alabama

Much of the news coverage in the days after Hurricane Katrina centered on the tragedy unfolding in New Orleans, but the suffering and devastation in Mississippi and Alabama were just as heartbreaking. Katrina claimed 220 lives in Mississippi. The storm also wiped out 90 percent of the buildings along the Biloxi-Gulfport coastline, displaced tens of thousands of people, severed bridges and highways, and cut power to about 800,000 customers. As in New Orleans, many people who did not evacuate the Mississippi coast were forced into attics and onto rooftops by rising waters. Many drowned inside flooded buildings, others were swept away by the storm surge that destroyed their houses, and a few were hit by falling debris kicked up by the hurricane-force winds. Compared with the stranded residents of New Orleans, a larger percentage of Mississippians who stayed behind had the vehicles or means to evacuate but chose not to, either because they were in frail health, refused to leave pets or businesses unprotected, or simply believed they could weather the storm.

Some of them were tragically mistaken. J. Anthony "Tony" Brugger, for example, refused to leave his Harbour Oaks Inn, a historic three-story bed-and-breakfast in Pass Christian that he and his wife had opened in 1992. The night before Hurricane Katrina made landfall, when asked why he was not evacuating, Brugger replied, "The house was built in 1860. We've got 15 years of sweat in it, restoring it. It was an old hotel, and it's been through some big storms. It's the highest spot in town. . . . So we can usually ride out the storm surge."[34] Brugger died the next morning amid Katrina's horrendous winds, as deadly waves crushed the inn to pieces in less than half an hour, leaving nothing intact but a concrete porch.

Katrina also caused significant misery in Alabama, where the state's second-largest city, Mobile, was inundated with floodwaters. Despite mandatory evacuation orders and the opening of eleven shelters, many people ignored warnings and decided to ride out the storm. At least two people were killed, and the hurricane's massive storm surge damaged many homes in south Mobile County's waterfront communities, leaving hundreds homeless. Derek Presley, a resident of the coastal area, found only a plaque that his grandmother had given him where his house once stood. "It's all that's left of my house,"[35] he said.

Altogether, the Katrina disaster caused tremendous suffering and stress not only for the multitudes of stranded New Orleans residents and people living on the coasts of Mississippi and Alabama, but also for many throughout the country. Indeed, people in the United States and around the world prayed for Katrina's victims and hoped that help would soon arrive.

3

Responding to the Crisis: Challenge and Controversy

AS THE THOUSANDS of people stranded in New Orleans and other stricken gulf coast zones endured days of terrible suffering, local, state, and federal officials slowly organized disaster aid and rescue efforts. Eventually victims of Hurricane Katrina were rescued and evacuated to safety. Most began to receive emergency aid. The plight of the storm victims, however, revealed deep faults in the government emergency response systems and created significant political fallout.

Communication and Transportation Problems

By any measure, the government response to the Katrina disaster was slow. Local and state officials had mobilized police and state National Guard troops to be ready when Katrina hit, but coordination of these local efforts soon became exceedingly difficult, for several reasons. One of the worst problems was that communications networks were disrupted or destroyed by the storm; officials on the scene had little ability to assess the damage, instruct emergency personnel, manage rescue efforts, or report to superiors in state capitals or Washington, D.C. First responders and other personnel turned to radios, but not everyone had radios, many radio frequencies were often jammed, and some radio transmitters had been destroyed by the storm. After the terrorist attacks

New Orleans residents are rescued by helicopter during the first days of September.

of September 11, 2001, Congress allocated funds to states to improve emergency communications systems, but Louisiana had yet to upgrade its equipment when Katrina struck. As a result, the best emergency communication devices—satellite phones—were not widely available in the state. Rescue workers were often forced to rely on low-tech methods, such as amateur ham radio operators or human runners, to relay messages.

The second most important resource —transportation—also was limited after the storm. In New Orleans, there simply were not enough boats, helicopters, buses, and other vehicles available to rescue and transport the tens of thousands who needed to be quickly evacuated. The resources of the Louisiana National Guard, already stretched thin by the deployment of more than three thousand of its members to Iraq, were further depleted when its local barracks flooded, destroying communications gear as well as twenty high-water trucks that would have been of great value in rescuing stranded citizens. Coast Guard helicopters and their crews were invaluable, but more rescue aircraft and pilots were needed. New Orleans airports were shut down, and there was a critical shortage of buses to evacuate people from the disaster zone to unaffected cities. Neither local, state, nor federal officials had enough buses in place before the storm, and once the storm's damage was done, the urgent effort to mobilize a fleet of buses and drivers took several days, hampered by the communication breakdowns and bus drivers' fears of looters and violence.

Their fears were not entirely unwarranted, as it became difficult to maintain law and order in New Orleans in the days after the disaster. When the looting and crime spree broke out, local police forces were short-staffed, overworked, and often outnumbered as they tried to regain control and restore calm. On Wednesday, August 31, National Guard troops were sent in to help the police, but this force, too, was not enough to control looting that was becoming increasingly hostile.

Criticism of Government Responses

Faced with these challenges and deteriorating conditions in overcrowded shelters, state and local officials were overwhelmed and quickly faced attack from the media and from each other. Critics blamed them for not issuing the mandatory evacuation order sooner and for failing to plan for the evacuation of poor people who could not help themselves before the storm. After the storm hit, critics said officials made confused decisions and failed to specify to the federal government what resources were needed. On Monday, August 29, for example, Governor Blanco of Louisiana had asked President Bush for "everything you've got"[36] without specifying what that meant. However, Louisiana politicians said that the disaster was simply too catastrophic to be handled without federal direction and help. As Andrew Kopplin, Blanco's chief of staff, explained, "This was a bigger natural disaster than any state could handle by itself, let alone a small state and a relatively poor one."[37]

Meanwhile, the Federal Emergency Management Agency (FEMA), the federal government's main disaster relief agency, seemed slow to grasp the full extent of the disaster. Both before and after the storm, the agency held back, expecting state and local officials to take the lead. FEMA even ordered emergency personnel to stay out of the stricken areas unless dispatched by those local authorities. A full five hours after the hurricane hit, FEMA chief Michael Brown finally asked Homeland Security director Michael Chertoff for permission to send a small force of a thousand relief workers to the gulf, but it was estimated that the group would not reach the disaster zone for forty-eight hours. Chertoff, for his part, did not declare Katrina "an incident of national significance," the designation that triggers a coordinated federal rescue and aid effort, until August 30, a full thirty-six hours after the storm hit. In general, the federal response proved to be too little, too late.

In this tense atmosphere, one of the most controversial charges was that the government responded slowly to the disaster because many of its victims were poor and black. In fact, in the worst-damaged area of New Orleans—the lower Ninth Ward—98 percent of the residents were African American and more than a third lived in poverty, but federal officials vehemently denied that racial discrimination was a factor in any part of the rescue and relief effort. Angry critics claimed, however, that these urban poor blacks did not support the Bush administration and were therefore treated indifferently in their time of crisis—even when federal aid did arrive, they charged, it focused on law-and-order concerns such as arresting looters rather than helping people in need. Civil rights activist the Reverend Jesse Jackson did not discount these inflammatory

Hundreds of homes in the lower Ninth Ward were completely flooded. Many homeowners had no choice but to wait on their roofs for help.

charges, stating, "Many black people feel that their race, their property conditions and their voting patterns have been a factor in the response."[38]

This issue was hotly debated; what almost everyone agreed on, however, was that FEMA prolonged people's suffering by failing to provide sufficient emergency aircraft, boats, and vehicles to get people out of flooded areas in a timely manner and by failing to quickly deliver food, water, and medical supplies to those who were stranded.

Ordinary Heroes

While they waited, forced to fend for themselves until help arrived, many people went to extraordinary lengths to help others. Doctors and nurses at area hospitals, for example, worked around the clock to save critically ill patients deprived of vital medicines and machinery. At New Orleans Methodist Hospital, part of the hospital's roof blew off, electricity was lost, and water flooded the hallways. Even after backup power sources failed, the staff stayed on the job. As Dr. Albert Barracas explained, "We lost our generator within 24 hours. We could not get fuel. We had to hand-bag ventilate patients [manually pump air in and out of patients' lungs]."[39]

As days passed, ordinary people also became extraordinarily resourceful, finding ingenious ways to help others without official aid. Two emergency workers reported the many kinds of generosity and quick thinking they witnessed:

> The maintenance workers who used a forklift to carry the sick and disabled. The engineers who rigged, nurtured and kept the generators running. The electricians who improvised thick extension cords stretching over blocks to share the little electricity we had in order to free cars stuck on rooftop parking lots. . . . Doormen who rescued folks stuck in elevators. Refinery workers who broke into boat yards, "stealing" boats to rescue their neighbors clinging to their roofs in flood waters. Mechanics who helped hotwire any car that could be found to ferry people out of the city. And the food service workers who scoured the commercial kitchens, improvising communal meals for hundreds of those stranded.[40]

Many police officers acted beyond the call of duty as well. More than a third of the New Orleans police force failed to report to duty after the storm, many choosing instead to stay with their families, so the on-duty force was stretched to the limit. Yet many dedicated police officers still worked twelve- to eighteen-hour days trying to maintain order and help survivors, in the face of flooded streets, no electricity, little fuel for transportation, communication breakdowns, scarce food, destroyed buildings, and a desperate, scared, and sometimes armed and hostile populace. Some officers simply could not take the pressure and walked off the job. At least two officers committed suicide, overwhelmed by despair, sorrow, and their own personal losses. As Detective Lawrence Dupree said, "If we really acted the way the situation dictated, we would all be killing ourselves. But we are making the best of a bad situation, and it's brought us closer together."[41]

Outside the disaster zone, countless numbers of people who had little themselves made room for relatives, friends, and strangers who had lost everything, providing them with food and shelter and other kinds of support until they could get back on their feet. Kirby Robinson, a resident of Houston, Texas, found himself housing twenty-seven Katrina victims in the week after the storm. First, he provided shelter for his childhood friend, Demond Lemon, and his family, who had been flooded out of their New Orleans home. Then, Robinson took in Lemon's mother and her friend, and later five children from Lemon's neighborhood. Soon, more friends and relatives called and Robinson could not turn them away, explaining, "If you have any space in your house, you should at least let 'em in."[42]

Pleas for Federal Help

After three days of chaos, on Wednesday, August 31, Governor Blanco pleaded with President Bush for more federal help, requesting 40,000 National Guard troops. The next day, Thursday, September 1, Nagin echoed Blanco's pleas, saying in a TV interview, "This is a desperate SOS. Right now we are out of resources at the convention center and

A Navy Hero

Navy captain Robert Lansden was one of the many heroes of Hurricane Katrina. He and his crew weathered the storm inside a disabled navy ship that was docked at the New Orleans port. Remarkably, the ship was not damaged and still had electricity, water, and—most important—771,000 gallons (2.9 million l) of precious diesel fuel. Lansden requested navy permission to use the ship as an emergency resource for storm victims. Deciding not to wait for official approval, however, he offered aid to nearby West Jefferson Medical Center, which was struggling to keep patients alive without electricity or running water. Forty patients with kidney failure were at severe risk because the dialysis unit, which acts as an artificial kidney and cleans the blood of toxins, could not be operated. Lansden and others managed to move both the patients and the center's huge dialysis machines on board the ship, and thanks to this quick action, the patients were saved. Meanwhile, with full permission from the navy, Lansden helped rig a method for siphoning the ship's fuel into tanker trucks so that it could be used to power hospitals and emergency vehicles during the first few harrowing days after the storm.

don't anticipate enough buses. We need buses. Currently the convention center is unsanitary and unsafe and we're running out of supplies."[43] Later that day, Nagin reiterated his call for help in an emotional radio interview:

> Excuse my French, everybody in America, but I am pissed. . . . I need reinforcements, I need troops, man. I need 500 buses. [Federal officials are] thinking small, man, and this is a major, major deal. God is looking down on this and if they are not doing everything in their power to save people, they are going to pay the price. Every day that we delay, people are dying, and they're dying by the hundreds, I'm willing to bet you. . . . Don't tell me 40,000 people are coming here. They're not here. It's too doggone late. Get off your asses and let's do something and let's fix the biggest goddamn crisis in the history of this country.[44]

In response to the growing criticism, federal officials mobilized transportation for evacuating stranded residents and ordered some thirty thousand National Guardsmen from around the country to the gulf coast region to stop the looting and restore order. The Pentagon also mounted a massive search-and-rescue operation, sending four navy ships loaded with helicopters, boats, troops, and emergency supplies. Still, such a large operation required time, and thousands of people remained stranded in their homes and other buildings, or trapped at the city's shelters, waiting without food or water for at least two more days. Touring the battered areas on Friday, September 2, the eve of Labor Day weekend, Bush publicly acknowledged that the government response was "not acceptable."[45]

The Cavalry Finally Arrives

Beginning on Friday, however, conditions slowly began to improve in the disaster areas. A convoy of military vehicles rolled into New Orleans and made its way to the Superdome and convention center to distribute food and water to the exhausted, angry crowds there. Over the next few days the newly arrived forces would hand out 620,000 bottles of water and 320,000 meals.

In a radio address on Saturday morning, September 3, Bush promised, "The federal government will do its part. Where our response is not working, we'll make it right. Where our response is working, we will duplicate it. We have a responsibility to our brothers and sisters all along the Gulf Coast, and we will not rest until we get this right and the job is done."[46]

On Saturday more than seven thousand active-duty troops from the 82nd Airborne Division, the First Cavalry, the First Marine Expeditionary Force, and the Second Marine Expeditionary Force arrived in Louisiana to assist in rescues and disaster relief. They joined the Coast Guard and a growing contingent of National Guard soldiers that soon exceeded twenty thousand. By the end of the day on Saturday, law enforcement officials announced at a press conference that the worst of the crime wave that broke out after Katrina was over. U.S. Attorney Jim Letten of New Orleans said, "We are taking the streets back. . . . The

streets of New Orleans belong to its citizens, not the violent thugs who have stuck their heads up out of holes in an attempt to exploit a tragedy."[47] State officials set up a temporary booking and detention center in downtown New Orleans that was capable of housing up to seven hundred people, and judges planned to set up a makeshift court. Together, local, state, and federal officials pledged that all violent offenders would soon be removed from the streets and that law and order would be restored to New Orleans.

Transportation, too, was finally coordinated. Over the next several days a fleet of buses removed people from overcrowded shelters to fully functioning shelters outside the disaster zone. An estimated fifteen thousand people were transported to the Houston Astrodome, 355 miles (571km) away, which Texas officials had quickly equipped as a temporary relocation site. Many other survivors traveled in

President George W. Bush surveyed the Gulf Coast from Air Force One on August 31, 2005.

Military patrols helped to reestablish order on the streets of New Orleans.

small groups to various other locations across the country. As word spread that there was at last a way out of the city, more and more people showed up at the Superdome and convention center asking to be evacuated. The buses ran day and night; in addition, many people were flown out of New Orleans by military and commercial aircraft or sent north on Amtrak trains. By the end of the Labor Day weekend, a week after Hurricane Katrina struck, both the ruined Superdome and the convention center were emptied of evacuees. On Monday, September 5, Blanco praised the emergency teams in New Orleans for making "outstanding progress."[48]

Despite the positive developments, however, many people were not yet out of danger. A stream of dislocated residents was still arriving at shelters by the hundreds, mostly on foot, to wait for a ride out of town, and approximately two thousand people, many with serious medical problems, remained in a terminal at the city's main airport, awaiting evacuation. An unknown number of victims also continued to cling to life inside buildings surrounded by water, wondering if and when help would arrive. As late as September 3, law enforcement agencies fielded one thousand distress calls from still-stranded citizens.

More FEMA Mismanagement

As the rescue mission began to relieve victims' immediate needs, attention turned to FEMA's mishandling of the continuing crisis. Critics claimed that FEMA was actually blocking some attempted relief missions. In one highly publicized incident, more than one thousand firefighters from around the country who volunteered to help rescue victims had been told to stay out of the gulf area and await FEMA orders. The group spent days stalled at an Atlanta airport, playing cards and taking classes on the history of FEMA. As one frustrated firefighter from Texas complained, "They've got people here who are search-and-rescue certified, paramedics, haz-mat [hazardous materials] certified . . . [and] we're sitting in here [in] class while there are still [victims] in Louisiana who haven't been contacted yet."[49] Finally, instead of being used to conduct desperately needed rescues, the firefighters were instructed that they would be community-relations officers for FEMA, sent to the gulf coast region to hand out fliers containing FEMA's phone number.

Aaron Broussard, president of Jefferson Parish, offered one of the most compelling public indictments of FEMA during a highly emotional interview on NBC's news discussion, *Meet the Press*, on Sunday, September 4. Broussard told moderator Tim Russert:

> We had Wal-Mart deliver three trucks of water, trailer trucks of water. FEMA turned them back. They said we didn't need them. This was a week ago. FEMA—we had 1,000 gallons of diesel fuel on a Coast Guard vessel docked in my parish. The Coast Guard said, "Come get the fuel right away." When

An estimated 15,000 Katrina evacuees were sheltered at the Houston Astrodome.

we got there with our trucks, they got word. "FEMA says don't give you the fuel." Yesterday—yesterday—FEMA comes in and cuts all of our emergency communication lines. They cut them without notice. Our sheriff, Harry Lee, goes back in, he reconnects the line. He posts armed guards on our line and says, "No one is getting near these lines." Sheriff Harry Lee said that if . . . [the] American government would have responded like Wal-Mart has responded, we wouldn't be in this crisis.[50]

In the face of such accusations, criticism of the federal government's response intensified. Republicans and Democrats alike, both inside and outside of government, called the emergency effort a national disgrace. Louisiana senator Mary L. Landrieu, for example, spoke out angrily about what she called "the staggering incompetence of the federal government."[51] Colin Powell, Bush's former secretary of state, admitted, "There have been a lot of failures at a lot of levels—local, state and federal."[52]

On September 9, the mounting criticism led to Michael Brown's removal as the director of FEMA's Katrina relief effort. He was replaced by Vice Admiral Thad W. Allen, chief of staff of the U.S. Coast Guard. Three days later Brown also resigned his position as director of FEMA. Despite these developments, though, the president's approval ratings dropped to a new low of 39 percent, with many citizens expressing concern about his leadership. A poll conducted by Pew Research Center, for example, found that 67 percent of Americans believed Bush could have done more to speed relief for Katrina's victims, and just 28 percent believed he did all he could. Under pressure, Bush took full responsibility for the federal government's failures and promised to investigate the government's response, and Congress began hearings on the matter.

FEMA administrator Michael Brown resigned in the face of mounting criticism of his leadership during the Katrina crisis.

Successes in the Relief Effort

Amid the criticism of relief efforts in Katrina's wake, however, there were some bright spots that the media sometimes overlooked. In fact, beginning on Monday, August 29, the day Hurricane Katrina hit land, and continuing over the next week, a broad-based, ad hoc rescue effort mounted by local, state, and federal responders pulled more than twenty-five thousand people to safety as floodwaters rose in New Orleans.

The first responders on the scene were dozens of Coast Guard helicopters, whose crews pulled thousands of people out of the water in the first couple of days and ultimately logged as many as fifty-five hundred rescues. The Coast Guard units were quickly joined by U.S. Air Force and Army helicopters, whose pilots flew numerous search-and-rescue missions and together saved more than fifteen hundred stranded flood victims. The Air National Guard, too, contributed helicopters. Altogether, 113 helicopters were in operation in the New Orleans region as of Thursday, September 1.

These early rescue missions were not coordinated by state or federal officials, and the pilots often had no ability to communicate even with each other. On their own, however, many responders showed great resourcefulness and efficiency. One example was the First Battalion, 244th Aviation Division in New Orleans, which had flown its seventeen UH-60 Black Hawk helicopters to Houston before Monday's storm, but returned to help with the rescue efforts later that day. To fit more people into the helicopter cabins on each search-and-rescue run, the crews removed the aircraft's seats. As Captain John Plunkett explained, "With the seats you could get 11, without them you could jam 31 inside. We didn't care if they were strapped in, we just wanted to get them out of harm's way."[53]

In addition to the air rescues, numerous boat rescues were conducted by the New Orleans police and fire departments. Police officers and firefighters managed to put

The Last Survivor

One of the last people rescued in the aftermath of Katrina was a tough, wiry seventy-six-year-old named Gerald Martin. On September 16, 2005, a full eighteen days after Katrina inundated the city, two California firefighters helping with house-to-house searches waded through the water to Martin's house, expecting to find only bodies. When they knocked down the front door, however, they found Martin quite alive, sitting on a chair in his water logged kitchen. Incredibly, he had survived for more than two weeks in his attic with only a 1.5-gallon (5.7 l) jug of water, from which he drank only a few gulps each day. By the time he was found, Martin was severely dehydrated and had lost a lot of weight, but otherwise was in good spirits. He told rescuers that he felt great but was a little thirsty, and he asked to be taken to Taco Bell for some fast food. Instead, his delighted rescuers quickly transferred Martin to a nearby hospital where he was fed and cared for and later reunited with his surprised and happy family.

Gerald Martin was rescued after surviving in his attic for eighteen days with less than two gallons of water.

about two hundred boats in the water within the first twenty-four hours after the flooding started. Even the Louisiana Fish and Wildlife Service pitched in to help. Exactly how many victims these responders saved is uncertain, but the total was likely in the thousands.

By the end of Labor Day weekend, very few stranded citizens remained to be saved, and many helicopter pilots and boat operators turned to other tasks, such as transporting supplies, dropping sandbags, and transporting people who were not threatened by floodwaters. With the immediate human crisis seemingly under control, however, officials and others turned to face the enormity of the damage wrought by Katrina.

4

Assessing the Damage

ONCE THE INITIAL shock of the Katrina disaster had subsided and the coordination of humanitarian relief efforts was well under way, officials and residents were forced to confront the storm's massive damage. The destruction included more than a thousand deaths, more than a million people displaced, catastrophic property losses, environmental damage, and a disrupted economy. And to make matters worse, another major hurricane headed toward the battered gulf coast only four weeks after Katrina's devastating strike.

Thousands of Evacuees

By early September, the first stage of disaster relief—evacuation of storm and flood victims—was well under way and most of those who had been trapped in flooded parts of New Orleans and other areas had been transported to safe locations. Almost sixty thousand storm victims were taken to shelters throughout Louisiana, and over two hundred thousand more were housed in shelters in other states across the nation, many in neighboring Texas. Uncounted others checked into hotels, found refuge at private or church-funded aid centers, or moved in with friends and relatives. In fact, aid workers and family experts say that, by far, the largest share of those displaced by Katrina were taken in by their extended families in Louisiana. Carl A. Brasseaux, a history professor at the University of Louisiana, offered this opinion of the role family would play: "There is no question that family has and will dwarf any other kind of assistance in this disaster. . . . Family ties are still stronger and more viable here than anywhere else in the United States."[54] The total number of persons displaced and made homeless by the storm, experts said, was staggering—more than a million.

Even after most stranded survivors had been rescued and moved from the stricken disaster area, however, as many as five thousand to ten thousand people still remained in New Orleans, many in dry areas of higher ground but a significant number in still-flooded low-lying areas, refusing all efforts to get them to evacuate. Some reportedly refused to leave their treasured pets, which were not permitted in many shelters. Others were cut off from news reports and had no idea how dangerous the flooding was and how severely damaged their community was. Some simply clung to their homes and independence, stubbornly resisting all appeals to leave. As one New Orleans

Some New Orleans residents, such as this woman, refused to evacuate their homes.

holdout named Loranger protested, "They can't throw me out of my house. I own property here, and I have dogs and stuff. . . . Isn't this still the United States of America?"[55]

In light of the vast damage and lack of services, Mayor Ray Nagin ordered the mandatory evacuation of all remaining people from New Orleans on Tuesday, September 6, instructing rescue teams to use force, if necessary, to get people out. Despite the order, however, rescue workers were reluctant to use physical force. Firm persuasion proved sufficient to convince most remaining residents to leave their homes with rescue workers, as long as pets could come too. Melvin Johnson, for example, who lived in a dry house in one of the few neighborhoods that largely escaped the flooding, initially refused to consider leaving because he could not abandon his two dogs. He promised, "They're going to have to drag me out kicking, screaming and fighting all the way."[56] But when arrangements were made to evacuate Johnson's dogs with him, he agreed to leave.

Stranded Pets and Animals

The issue of pets and other animal victims of Katrina, in fact, attracted much attention in the weeks following the storm. Animal rights advocates and ordinary pet lovers across the country questioned why rescuers refused to allow people to take their pets to shelters. In one well-publicized incident, a police officer took a small dog from the arms of a scared little boy waiting to get on a bus to be evacuated from New Orleans. The boy cried out, "Snowball! Snowball!"[57] as he was separated from his pet and then became so agitated that he vomited. Concerned citizens who were moved by the emotional scene offered a reward for the dog, and fortunately, days later, state veterinarians announced that Snowball had been found and would be returned to the boy, who was now at a shelter in Texas. Later evacuees were sometimes allowed to take along their small pets, but rescuers generally refused to permit large or aggressive dogs, citing safety concerns and the limitations of shelter resources.

The policy, critics said, probably resulted in many human deaths when people chose to stay in their homes rather than abandon their pets. In addition, for the many thousands of other evacuees who did leave their pets as instructed, expecting to return to care for them in a few days at most, the policy created some of the most emotionally painful scenes of the post-Katrina period. As many as fifty thousand dogs, cats, birds, reptiles, and other pet animals were either locked in flooded homes or stranded outside to die slowly without food or clean water. As reporters Reed Johnson and Steven Barrie-Anthony wrote in the September 8 *Los Angeles Times*,

> Some [pets] are still grimly hanging onto life. They sit forlornly on the rooftops of flooded homes, slowly starving to death as rescuers in boats ignore them, looking for people instead. Some have even tried swimming to boats, only to be rebuffed. Many other pets didn't make it, and their bodies now lie in pools of scummy water or by the side of highways.[58]

When evacuees discovered that they would not be able to return to retrieve their pets, many began pleading for the Humane Society and other animal protection groups to rescue their animals. These groups tried to mount a quick rescue effort, but state and federal officials prevented them from going into flooded areas during the first few days of the disaster. Eventually, pet rescue operations did begin, but by then many animals had suffered terribly and rescuers had to race to save as many as they could. As Wayne Pacelle, president of the Humane Society of the United States, said, "The clock is really ticking. It's tearing us up knowing that so many animals are in need and [we] can't get to every one on our own."[59]

Thousands of pets were ultimately saved and sent to shelters, where workers planned to reunite them with their owners. Emergency workers also rescued many stranded horses and mules used to pull the tourist carriages that were a fixture in pre-Katrina New Orleans. Many more animals, however, could not be reached before they died or could not be corralled once they were found. Some of the

Flooding at the New Orleans Aquarium

Animals of all kinds suffered in the Katrina disaster. Along with untold numbers of household pets, some of the city's zoo animals died, as did most of the fish at the New Orleans aquarium. Opened in 1990, the Audubon Aquarium of the Americas was home to more than six thousand specimens of sea life. The aquarium was built to survive hurricanes, with tank walls 1 foot (0.3m) thick and windows designed to withstand winds of 140 miles (225km) per hour. It was equipped with a backup diesel generator to filter tank water and pump oxygen into fish tanks even after the electricity failed, and a group of volunteers even stayed during the storm to care for the aquarium's animals. The poststorm flooding, however, forced the evacuation of all staff, and by the time anyone could return, the generator motor had burnt out and most of the fish had died from lack of oxygen. Sharks, angelfish, sea horses, jellyfish, stingrays, and piranhas were all lost, but a few miracles were found alive—including two sea otters, nineteen penguins, an anaconda snake, a group of macaws, delicate sea dragons, a white alligator, and King Midas, a 250-pound (114kg) sea turtle.

This white alligator was moved to a facility in New Jersey after the New Orleans aquarium was damaged in the storm.

most difficult to catch were frightened cats, who often tried to hide from rescue workers. Also difficult to rescue were large dogs, many of whom banded together to form skittish dog packs that roamed the abandoned areas. As weeks passed, these stray dogs became gaunt and sick from lack of food and from drinking contaminated water. Unless they could be caught, most were not expected to live.

Recovering Bodies

As the search for human and animal survivors continued, emergency personnel began to focus their efforts on the grim task of recovering the bodies of people who died during the storm, the flooding, or the aftermath. In New Orleans, crews began a house-to-house search, marking the houses with spray paint to denote the number of "DB" (dead bodies) inside. By the time this recovery effort began, however, many of the bodies had been lying in the oppressive heat and humidity for days and were so decomposed and bloated that they were unrecognizable. Officials denied press coverage of the recovery work out of respect for the dead and their loved ones.

Many of the dead were elderly victims who were not evacuated in time from nursing homes. In St. Rita's Nursing Home in St. Bernard Parish, thirty-four swollen bodies were found amid the water and muck. Sadly, most of the elderly patients apparently drowned while trying to defend themselves against the rising waters. There was evidence that they tried to nail a table against one window, block another window with a table and an electric wheelchair, and push a couch against a door. They ran out of time and air, however,

Most dogs were not permitted into shelters following Katrina, forcing them to fend for themselves in the flooded conditions.

when the water rose almost to the ceiling. Days after the bodies were found, the owners of the nursing home were charged with thirty-four counts of negligent homicide for failing to evacuate despite severe storm warnings.

Initially, Nagin predicted as many as ten thousand dead, but early search results suggested that the actual total would be far less than that estimate. Blanco announced her great relief, stating, "We didn't lose as many lives as had been predicted, although we're still in the process of finding those we lost."[60] The death toll across the affected gulf coast, however, slowly rose as weeks passed. By late October, Louisiana's death toll stood at 1,053, while officials reported 228 deaths in Mississippi, 14 in Florida, 2 in Alabama, and 2 in Georgia. The dead were taken to two massive warehouses in Louisiana and Mississippi, where DNA analysis was used to identify them. Their grieving families, many of whom were already coping with homelessness and other major losses, had to wait until this long identification process was completed before they could retrieve and bury their lost loved ones.

Draining the Water

Alongside rescue and recovery teams, emergency crews set to work to drain the floodwaters from low-lying areas. On Sunday, September 4, the U.S. Army Corps of Engineers closed the main break in the canal flood walls by dropping about seven hundred 3,000-pound (1,362kg) sandbags into the gap. Engineers then made repairs to levee sections damaged by the storm surge. Once the levees were secure, the process of pumping out the approximately 800,000 acre-feet (9.9 million cubic m) of water from the city could begin. More than twenty-four temporary pumps were shipped to the region, and by Tuesday, September 6, a few of the city's forty pumping stations were restarted. Ever so slowly, the waters in New Orleans began to recede.

This procees required workers from the city's Sewerage and Water Board to work almost around the clock. Hurricane Katrina had flooded almost the entire pumping and

drainage system in the city, including the water system's main power plant. In the eastern part of the city, where the worst flooding occurred, one power station was completely underwater and not expected to return to service perhaps for months. Before workers could get pumps running, the pump engines had to be dried and cleaned. Even after pump function was restored, however, many pumps became clogged by debris or failed because of damaged electrical connections. Some workers, finding the pressure and safety risks intolerable, walked off the job. As Jason Higginbotham, the Water Board's emergency manager, said, "You could write a book about what these guys have been through."[61]

Officials initially predicted that pumping out the city could take three to six months, but this conservative estimate was quickly revised downward to about eighty days and then sharply down again with the remarkable success of the pumping effort. By mid-September most low-lying areas that had been almost completely underwater once again became visible and started to dry out.

An Environmental Catastrophe

As pumping progressed, new concerns arose over environmental damage caused by the storm. The water covering the city was polluted with what some called a "witches' brew" of raw sewage, bacteria, heavy metals, pesticides, toxic chemicals, and leaked oil. After this toxic soup was pumped out, a foul, equally toxic sludge was left behind.

The pollutants came from various sources, because Katrina struck one of the most industrialized parts of the country. In addition to the raw human waste that was released when all of New Orleans' sewage plants were flooded, as much as 7 million gallons (26.5 million l) of oil may have leaked from industrial plants, storage depots and other facilities—about two-thirds as much oil as spilled in the historic *Exxon Valdez* tanker oil spill in Alaska in 1989. Numerous other chemicals and fuels were added to the mix when the waters flooded many of the city's manufacturers, small businesses, and at least one large hazardous waste site. In addition, officials said that submerged homes were a likely

Floodwater was pumped out of New Orleans into Lake Pontchartrain. By mid-September 2005, most of the city was drying out.

The EPA found dangerous levels of E. coli bacteria and other toxins in the New Orleans floodwater.

source of cleaning products, pesticides, and other potentially hazardous materials commonly found in garages or under kitchen sinks. As New Orleans resident Jason Davis warned, "I saw a couple of dead rats, and if it's killing rats, it's bad."[62]

Tests conducted by the Environmental Protection Agency (EPA) in residential areas of New Orleans in the days after the flooding soon confirmed the presence of dangerous levels of *E. coli* bacteria, an indicator of human waste contamination, as well as certain viruses, a type of cholera-like bacteria, and high levels of lead, poisonous to humans. Officials also said the water contained hazardous petrochemical by-products, signaled by obvious oil and gasoline slicks visible on the water's surface. Later tests confirmed the presence of these and many other hazardous chemicals. Environmentalists and government officials expressed concern that the brackish water posed a great health risk to rescue workers and people still living in, or returning to, their flooded homes. Many of those evacuated from the area were already suffering from skin infections and diarrhea. Some scientists warned that dried-out toxic matter would break down into dust and become airborne, creating an even greater respiratory hazard. EPA administrator Stephen L. Johnson admitted, "This is the largest natural disaster that we believe the U.S. Environmental Protection Agency and nation has faced."[63]

To clear the flooded city, these polluted and bacteria-filled waters were pumped back into Lake Pontchartrain, where they threatened to poison the lake's fish population and turn the lake into a virtual cesspool long into the future. Because the lake is actually part of a vast estuary system connected to the Gulf of Mexico, experts worried that the toxic waters would make their way into the gulf waters, endangering fisheries, fragile coastal marshes, and the ocean ecosystem. Already, hundreds of miles of gulf coastline had been eroded by the storm, which destroyed much of the wetland habitat, reduced the size of marine and wildlife refuges in Louisiana, and made New Orleans and neighboring areas even more vulnerable to future storms. Various environmental agencies began studies to evaluate the full extent of the water and coastal damage.

Some local officials, however, optimistically predicted that nature would eventually take care of the pollution caused by the disaster. The lake, they said, is fed by several rivers and flushed regularly by tides from the gulf. Once in the ocean, pollutants would be widely dispersed. As Michael D. McDaniel, the Louisiana secretary of environmental quality, explained, "The wonderful thing about nature is its resilience. . . . The bacterial contaminants will not last a long time in the lake. They actually die off pretty fast. The organic material will degrade with natural processes. Metals will probably fall and be captured in the sediments. Nature does a good job. It just takes awhile."[64]

Property Damage

As the waters receded, the massive damage to property became achingly apparent. Between 150,000 and 200,000 homes in New Orleans were completely destroyed in the disaster, along with businesses of every kind and size. While some old New Orleans neighborhoods on higher ground, such as the historic French Quarter, survived with relatively minor damage, virtually no property in low-lying areas was left unscathed. The same was true in Mississippi, where Katrina wiped out 80 miles (129km) of coastline, destroyed about one-third of the homes in the state's six southernmost counties, and left another third severely damaged. Mobile, Alabama, also suffered major flood damage. Throughout the region, block after block of houses were ruined—some knocked down, some stripped to their studs, and many caked with a thick, stinking sludge of toxic mud and oil. Mixed in with the construction debris were shreds of furniture, household appliances, and every kind of personal possession, from clothing to photographs to CDs.

Many of the houses in New Orleans and Mississippi, experts said, were not salvageable and would have to be bulldozed. Indeed, almost everything that was covered by water—not only houses, but also ruined cars, shipping containers full of rotting meat and produce, freight trains, buses, sunken boats, schools, businesses, trees, and landscaping—would have to be torn apart and somehow disposed of. Many items could be recycled, but the rest would have to be either buried, burned, hauled away, or dumped into the sea.

Swiss Reinsurance Company, one of the world's largest insurers, predicted that property insurance claims would be at least $40 billion—a figure that would make Katrina the world's costliest hurricane. Total property losses, including private homes and commercial buildings that were not covered by insurance, and public properties, were expected to rise much higher, perhaps as high as $100 billion.

Economic Damage

The gulf economy was another victim of the hurricane and flooding. Thousands of local businesses, both large and small, shut down when Katrina hit, as factories, showrooms, and stores were destroyed by winds and

The beach town of Waveland, Mississippi, was leveled by Hurricane Katrina.

flooding. Coastal fishing enterprises were virtually destroyed, and farmland and cattle ranches, too, were wiped out. Even businesses that survived faced tough times ahead, especially tourist-related companies, because their customers had largely disappeared. In addition, infrastructure necessary for shipping and commerce, such as roads and bridges, suffered more than $10 billion in damage, further limiting the ability of local industries to bounce back from the disaster.

Economists said that it would take months for many businesses to reopen and that some might never recover. In southeastern Louisiana and coastal Mississippi, for example, the storm all but closed down the $2.75 billion-a-year commercial fishing industry. With their boats destroyed, docks washed away, shrimp habitat and oyster beds severely damaged, and waters contaminated by bacteria and chemicals, many small shrimp and oyster fishermen wondered how they would survive. As Jimmy Morgan, a Mississippi oyster fisherman like his father and grandfather, explained, "It don't get any worse than this. Nobody has anything left to fish with, even if the grounds was open."[65] Officials agreed, admitting it could be months or even years before area fishermen are back in business.

The economic effects of the Katrina disaster were also felt outside the gulf region. On its path across the gulf, the hurricane crossed directly over more than nine hundred oil and gas platforms, damaging many. Even production and refining facilities that were not damaged were shut down because they had no electrical power after the storm. Altogether the gulf facilities accounted for about 8 percent of total U.S. refining capacity, so their shutdown immediately caused a sharp spike in the cost of gasoline, sending average prices at the pump to more than three dollars per gallon across the nation.

The rising fuel costs were expected to slow the national economy, as producers of various goods raised prices to cover the increased shipping costs and consumers reduced spending to pay for the higher costs of commuting. Energy companies rushed to inspect and repair damaged facilities, but the government predicted it would take months for gas and oil production to rebound to its pre-Katrina levels, reach wholesalers, and have any impact on prices.

Hurricane Rita

Incredibly, just as New Orleans and surrounding areas began to assess the damage from Hurricane Katrina, another storm came barreling toward the Gulf of Mexico in late September, threatening the region with even more devastation. The new hurricane, named Rita, followed a path similar to Katrina's, across Florida and into the warm gulf waters. By Wednesday, September 24, Rita had grown as big as Katrina—a Category 5 storm with sustained winds of 175 miles (282km) per hour. It headed toward western Louisiana and Texas, sending residents scrambling to evacuate. Among those fleeing from Rita were thousands of storm-weary victims of Hurricane Katrina who had taken shelter in Texas.

Rita, however, slowed significantly as it approached the coast, hit less populated areas, and, though deadly, caused

Lessons Learned from Katrina

Embarrassed by criticism of their preparation for and response to Hurricane Katrina, government agencies took the next big storm, Hurricane Rita, very seriously. As Rita approached, federal officials sent troops and supplies to the gulf region much earlier than they did before Katrina and made sure to coordinate more closely with local authorities. President Bush also was publicly involved, closely monitoring the storm's approach and the federal government's disaster preparations. Local government officials, too, applied the experiences from Katrina to order evacuations early and provide buses to evacuate those who could not get out on their own.

Only one major problem surfaced during the preparations for Hurricane Rita—millions rushing to evacuate Houston and other threatened areas created a massive traffic jam that brought traffic on outbound freeways to a standstill. Some critics said officials were too slow to turn all freeway lanes into outbound, or northbound, lanes.

Disaster experts also suggested that gasoline trucks and other supplies should have been stationed along evacuation routes to help those who ran out of gas, food, or water during the mass exodus. Together, Katrina and Rita provided many important disaster preparation lessons for storms to come.

After watching the destruction caused by Katrina, Houston residents were quick to evacuate as Hurricane Rita approached.

only a fraction of the damage inflicted by Katrina. Rita was blamed for less than a hundred storm-related deaths. Nevertheless, Rita hit many offshore oil drilling rigs and production platforms, again disrupting the gulf's oil and gas production, and caused at least $5 billion in property damage to certain rural areas of Louisiana and Texas that Katrina missed. In addition, the rainfall from Rita was enough to cause water to crest over some of the recently repaired levees in New Orleans, once again flooding one of the hardest-hit, though now empty, neighborhoods in the city. As Major Barry Guidry of the National Guard put it, "Our worst fears came true."[66]

After Rita, therefore, the gulf region faced an expanded swath of destruction. One month after Katrina, and days after Rita, New Orleans and surrounding areas were just beginning to take the first steps on what promised to be a very long journey of recovery.

5

Moving Forward

THE NEXT CHAPTER in the story of the Katrina/Rita disaster involved the long-term effects of the twin storms. After the criticism of its early disaster relief efforts, the federal government sought to redeem itself by providing funds and temporary housing for the many gulf hurricane victims. Next came the cleanup, a messy and massive process accompanied by many environmental and health risks. Eventually, residents and officials began to turn their attention to the huge tasks of reconstruction and preventing similarly catastrophic damage from future storms. Even the most optimistic observers admitted that this extremely difficult process is likely to take many years.

Money for Rebuilding

As the short-term phase of disaster relief came to a close, the country prepared for the long-term recovery and rebuilding phase. In early September, the federal government authorized more than $62 billion in spending to begin this recovery process, but officials predicted that total costs could rise as high as $200 billion, roughly twice as much as the entire cost of the Marshall Plan, which rebuilt much of devastated Western Europe after World War II. The money was to be used in Louisiana to rebuild and upgrade the levees around New Orleans, repair highways and infrastructure, attract business development, and rebuild the city's destroyed residential areas. Parts of Mississippi, Alabama, and Texas would need similar investments to return to normal.

Despite the strong urge to restore the gulf region, however, many citizens and lawmakers worried about where this money would come from. Such generous government spending, critics pointed out, would force huge increases in the federal budget deficit, already growing because of the wars in Afghanistan and Iraq and large tax cuts promoted by the Bush administration. As budget analyst Stanley Collender said, "Katrina could easily become a milestone in the history of the federal budget."[67]

The issue soon sparked intense political debate as Democrats and Republicans began proposing very different ways of paying for Katrina. Many Democrats wanted to scale back Bush's tax cuts; some Republicans proposed canceling a Medicare prescription drug program enacted in 2003. Bush rejected tax increases but did not specify the source of the funds, maintaining only that "it's going to cost whatever it costs . . . but I am confident we can handle it."[68]

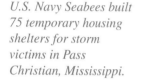

U.S. Navy Seabees built 75 temporary housing shelters for storm victims in Pass Christian, Mississippi.

Resettling Katrina Evacuees

Even as questions were raised about Katrina spending, however, pressing needs forced the federal government to begin dispersing funds. The first priority was providing housing and related assistance to the more than three hundred thousand Katrina and Rita evacuees still housed in temporary shelters. The poorest of these beleaguered victims received food and other necessities of life at the shelters, but as weeks passed, people grew tired of the lack of independence and privacy. Most evacuees were desperate to return to their homes or find permanent housing so they could start rebuilding their lives.

As a start, the Federal Emergency Management Agency (FEMA) began issuing $2,000 in emergency funds to eligible evacuees during the weeks after the disaster. The money enabled people to buy food, clothes, medicines, and other personal necessities, giving many new hope. As Astrodome shelter evacuee Percell Ford said, "This is a blessing, a true blessing, and it's going to help a lot of poor people. . . . Most of these folks are working people. They're ready to help themselves, but they need a start."[69] This initial cash grant program, however, was discontinued on September 26, following numerous distribution problems and computer glitches. It was followed by a new Transitional Housing Assistance Program that gave qualified recipients an additional $2,358 cash advance for three months' rent. As of late September, FEMA approved 253,000 applications for these grants, for a total expenditure of about $600 million. Under the new program, hurricane victims can continue to receive additional housing grants for eighteen months, up to a maximum of $26,200.

These measures, however, were insufficient to house the thousands of evacuees who wanted to stay in the gulf region, because there simply were not enough vacant rental houses after the storm. FEMA came under considerable criticism for wasting federal funds in making one hastily arranged deal on September 1, at the peak of the crisis: The agency agreed to pay what many called an exorbitant $236 million to lease three cruise ships from Carnival Cruise

Lines to house evacuees for up to six months (at an estimated cost of more than $1,280 per person per week, more than actual cruise passengers paid for vacation service). By late September fewer than eighteen hundred people (including many rescue workers) were still berthed on the ships.

Also, FEMA was authorized to spend $2 billion more to position up to fifty thousand mobile homes in state parks and on vacant lands throughout the region, with most of the units going to Louisiana. Although this housing effort was criticized for proceeding very slowly, temporary housing was the best solution for many until permanent housing could be built in New Orleans and other stricken areas, a process that experts said could take at least three to five years and maybe longer.

Middle-Class Victims

Many middle-class home owners who escaped the storm on their own and did not qualify for government assistance turned instead to their insurance policies. Property insurers typically assess the damage to homes caused by many kinds of perils and determine home owners' entitlement to insurance benefits. In many cases insurance will cover part or all of the cost of replacing destroyed homes and cars, and in some cases coverage includes living expenses while policyholders are uprooted. Insurance claims processing for the huge Hurricane Katrina disaster was slow, however. In the interim, many evacuees were forced to spend their savings or charge basic necessities such as hotel bills, food, gas, and clothing to credit cards.

The biggest obstacle to insurance reimbursement was that most private insurance policies do not cover flood damage. Only about 40 percent of New Orleans home owners had purchased separate flood insurance policies offered by the federal government. The situation of displaced rental tenants was no better, since few were expected to have renter's insurance that would cover their Katrina expenses or losses.

Those who find themselves unable to manage their rising debts after Katrina may face new obstacles. Many will

likely be barred from filing for bankruptcy, under a tough new bankruptcy law that took effect on October 17, 2005. The new law demands strict proof of inability to pay debts, requires credit counseling, and favors repayment over complete debt forgiveness. Some lawmakers tried to amend the law to provide for the Katrina situation, but that effort was defeated in Congress. Despite the planned government expenditures, therefore, Katrina was expected to leave a trail of financial hardship and ruin for middle-class as well as poverty-stricken victims.

New Orleans residents who took refuge in an elementary school await evacuation.

Nevertheless, middle-class, mostly white evacuees seemed in general to have had more control and choices after Katrina than poor, mostly black evacuees. Many had cars in which to escape the storm and could pay for hotel rooms and food while deciding what to do or while waiting for their insurance claims to be processed. Quite a few middle-class evacuees also managed to travel back to their flooded neighborhoods in their cars or rented boats to retrieve animals or items of sentimental value from their damaged homes. As reporters David Zucchino and Solomon Moore put it, "In the tragedy of New Orleans, there are two

Katrina survivors attend a temporary tent school in New Jersey just nine days after the hurricane.

classes of evacuees: those with means and mobility, and those without."[70]

Rebuilding Lives

Whether rich or poor, however, all evacuees faced the difficult challenge of building new lives, often in places far removed from the region they once called home. The first priority for many families was education. Enrolling children in school was an important step toward normalcy amid what had become a chaotic existence after Katrina. However, most schools in New Orleans and other hard-hit areas in the gulf were damaged or leveled in the disaster, displacing as many as two hundred thousand students. A few schools in the Algiers district reopened in September, but officials said schools in the eastern parts of the city would be closed for at least a year. In addition, many evacuees had scattered with their children to shelters across the country. As a result, many parents enrolled their children in new, unfamiliar schools, even temporarily, to interrupt their education as little as possible.

Parents, meanwhile, worried about how they would earn a living in the days ahead. The business shutdowns caused by the disaster left hundreds of thousands of people not only homeless, but also jobless, with few prospects for near-term work. In New Orleans alone, officials said, about 750,000 workers would be unable to return to their jobs for at least several months. In addition, the city was forced to lay off more than three thousand city workers after the storm because it could no longer afford to pay them. Once people and businesses return to the area and begin to rebuild their properties, officials expect a Katrina construction boom that should provide many short-term jobs. Long-term work, however, would have to await the city's rebuilding.

For many, experts predicted, this process of coping with the very real problems created by the disaster will be extremely difficult. Survivors who lost everything—loved ones, pets, homes, and jobs—may find the emotional trauma overwhelming. Children were especially vulnerable. One little girl in a Houston shelter, for example, had watched her mother drown in front of her as the waters rose. She drew a picture of heaven, with a note to her mother saying, "I'll see you in the white clouds."[71] As David Fassler, a psychiatrist at the University of Vermont, explained, "Kids have lost their homes, their schools, their neighborhoods, connections with friends. . . . I would expect to see an increase in anxiety, sleep difficulties, fears."[72] True recovery for Katrina's victims is expected to take many years.

Going Home

While many evacuees struggled to resettle, others focused on returning to their flooded homes. Even before the flooding receded, Mayor Nagin pressed to reopen as much of New Orleans as he could as quickly as possible. On September 15, Nagin announced a plan to allow as much as one-third of the population to return to certain sections of the city, such as Algiers, Uptown, and the French Quarter, that suffered minimal storm damage. In addition, Nagin said that the city's downtown would be opened to business owners. Nagin even promised that residents of completely flooded neighborhoods would soon be permitted to return, at least to check on their properties and remove personal items.

Nagin's plan, however, was criticized by federal officials, who were concerned about the polluted environment, the lack of power and clean water, and the absence of medical facilities. A second mandatory evacuation caused by the arrival of Hurricane Rita temporarily silenced the debate, but, immediately after the new storm, officials once again opened parts of the city to residents while cautioning them about health hazards. Nagin explained, "With Hurricane Rita behind us, the task at hand is to bring New Orleans back. . . . We want people to return and help us rebuild the city. However, we want everyone to assess the risks and make an informed decision about re-entry plans."[73]

Many evacuees gladly accepted the risks and returned to their once-flooded properties, but most faced new shock and grief when they found only rubble and sludge. Linda Griffiths, a grandmotherly resident from St. Bernard's Parish, got the first look at her house in late September. Surveying the damage, Griffiths said, "There's just nothing to salvage, nothing." After repeated forays into the mud, however, Griffiths found a silver tray her parents owned, a few bracelets, and even a lockbox containing her important papers. She concluded, "I'll be back. . . . I was born here, raised here, my daddy is buried here and I will be too. It may take years, but I'm coming back home."[74]

Restoring Infrastructure and Services

Mayor Nagin also pushed to get New Orleans's transportation systems and services back in operation quickly after the disaster. The city's busy international airport resumed cargo flights on September 11 and some passenger service on September 13. The New Orleans port, too, reopened in

Aid from Around the World

The United States is traditionally known as a prosperous country that rushes to other countries' aid after natural disasters. In a reversal of this scenario, donations of aid and disaster supplies poured into the United States from around the world as news of the Katrina disaster spread. Altogether ninety-four different countries promised aid. The largest offer of $500 million came from oil-rich Kuwait. Another wealthy oil nation, Qatar, offered $100 million. Canada pledged $5 million in disaster relief and sent ships loaded with soldiers to help in the relief efforts. China, too, offered $5 million in aid and, along with many other countries, offered items such as generators, food, tents, blankets, drinking water, and medical supplies. Germany sent disaster experts, evacuation aircraft, water purification equipment, and high-speed pumps to pump water out of New Orleans. The Netherlands, which itself lies below sea level, offered to help New Orleans plan against future flooding. In moving gestures, even some of the world's poorest countries, such as Sri Lanka, Afghanistan, and Bangladesh, pledged what they could, and a longtime U.S. enemy, Cuba, offered to send more than a thousand doctors in a humanitarian mission to the gulf coast.

Many nations offered assistance to the United States in the aftermath of Katrina. In this photo, relief materials bound for the Gulf Coast are loaded onto a plane in Beijing.

mid-September, although storm damage to facilities and the loss of workers were expected to delay resumption of normal capacity for at least six months.

In addition, in negotiations that took just four hours, the city contracted to begin rebuilding a section of Interstate 10, the area's main freeway. The construction company that won the $30 million bid was given just forty-five days to complete one set of lanes and a bonus of $75,000 for each day the job is finished ahead of schedule.

Meanwhile, utility workers worked around the clock to restore the area's electricity and other utilities—tasks made extremely difficult by the enormous storm and flood damage. Most areas, for example, first had to be cleared of

Some businesses in the French Quarter of New Orleans were cleaned up and reopened within a month of the disaster.

trees and rubble and then were rewired for electricity, block by block, house by house. Even after power was restored to a street, each house had to be inspected for safety before crews would turn on the electricity. The process was also slow for other services, such as sewage, water, phones, and high-speed Internet. As a result, neighborhoods on higher ground with limited damage, such as the French Quarter and the Central Business District, soon enjoyed electricity, clean water, a functioning sewage system, and in some places phone and Internet service, while much of the eastern part of the city was expected to remain without many of those services for much longer. Months after Katrina, for example, low-lying regions such as the lower Ninth Ward still lacked electricity and running water.

Cleaning Up

Gulf coast officials also began planning the arduous job of bulldozing ruined buildings and clearing the debris caused by the storm and flooding. This cleanup was expected to create a huge volume of trash. Experts said that all the downed trees, ruined carpets, moldy drywall, and damaged furniture and appliances will create as much as 55 million cubic yards (42 million cu m) of debris in Louisiana, 50 million cubic yards (38 million cu m) in Mississippi, and 2 million cubic yards (1.5 million cu m) in Alabama—enough to fill 6 million dump trucks. Added to that will be more than 163,000 flooded cars and 93,000 sunken boats that must be scrapped.

The job is expected to take up to two years at a minimum cost of $2 billion. Witnesses to the damage are not surprised by these projections. As local reporters James Varney and Jan Moller explained,

> Even a cursory glance at the landscape in New Orleans . . . shows how daunting the task will be. In many areas back roads remain impassable, and in some neighborhoods bags of rotting food and other foul-smelling materials are piled indiscriminately. Cars are smashed, waterlogged, and left everywhere. Businesses are without windows, with glass shards scattered about parking lots and sidewalks.[75]

Much of the processing time will involve separating the debris for recycling and monitoring it for toxic chemicals. Crews will first remove and recycle organic matter, such as the tree branches and trunks that clog public highways and properties. Next comes the time-consuming job of clearing, sorting, and recycling nonorganic and potentially toxic debris from private property. Unfortunately for those trying to stay in their homes, removing the smelly piles of rotting curbside trash from residential areas is last on the schedule.

Economic Renewal

After the huge cleanup effort, residents, business owners, and officials must undertake the even more monumental task of reconstruction. The first step in the rebuilding process will be getting businesses to return to the region to provide good sources of jobs and revenue. To encourage business investment in Louisiana, Governor Blanco asked for the federal government's help and proposed a rebuilding package designed to convince the business community that relocating in New Orleans would be safe and profitable. One strategy proposed by the state is to provide financial inducements to businesses, such as tax credits, grants, and low-cost loans. The governor also asked for monies for local governments whose tax bases were eroded by the depopulation caused by the storm and flooding. These monies would be used to cover the costs of police, firefighters, utility workers, and other local government employees until the area recovers.

According to the governor, however, the most essential part of the proposed package is building an improved levee system that would protect New Orleans against future flooding. Unless new legislation provides otherwise, the U.S. Army Corps of Engineers has authority to rebuild the levees only to their pre-Katrina condition, a level designed to protect the city from a Category 3 hurricane. This type of reconstruction, local officials argued, is proceeding too slowly and will be a wasted effort against another Category 4 or 5 storm. Louisiana representatives instead pushed for

Disaster Spending: Honest and Fair?

Part of the controversy surrounding the government response to Hurricane Katrina involved the bidding process for disaster relief and rebuilding contracts. Charges of political favoritism arose soon after FEMA began issuing multimillion-dollar contracts in the weeks after the storm. Critics pointed out that more than 80 percent of the contracts, worth $1.5 billion, signed by FEMA for Katrina work before the end of September were awarded with little or no competitive bidding.

Moreover, many of the companies receiving large government contracts had political connections. One big contractor, AshBritt, had paid $40,000 for lobbying services in 2005 to a firm founded by Mississippi governor Haley Barbour; it received contracts worth $568 million for trash removal. Two other major contractors that also won multimillion-dollar deals—the Shaw Group, and Kellogg, Brown & Root—had hired Joseph Allbaugh, President Bush's former campaign manager and the former head of FEMA, to help them get federal contracts. After much criticism, the new director of FEMA, R. David Paulison, announced in October 2005 that all of the no-bid contracts would be rebid competitively in order to restore public confidence in the agency.

the president to appoint a special commission that could more quickly rebuild a levee system designed to withstand Category 5 storms.

Mississippi governor Barbour and Alabama governor Bob Riley echoed Blanco's pleas for federal rebuilding aid. Both endorsed the idea of business tax write-offs, and Riley also urged lawmakers to resolve the escalating dispute over whether flood damages should be covered by private hurricane insurance. The U.S. Congress is expected to consider all these ideas as it crafts a long-term package to help all the gulf coast states recover and rebuild.

Rebuilding New Orleans and Vicinity

Rebuilding New Orleans and surrounding areas, by all accounts, will pose one of the biggest challenges the country has ever faced. Peter H. King reported in the *Los Angeles Times* some of the tough questions raised by the prospect of rebuilding New Orleans:

Who will pay for it? How does a city function when more than half of it has been turned into a public works project of Hoover Dam proportions? Where will the workers to do this rebuilding live? Who will those workers be? Can the . . . charm of New Orleans . . . be recreated, or is much of the [city] doomed to a future of tiled-roof housing tracts and fashion malls? How much of the lowlying city should be rebuilt? Can the defenses against future hurricanes be shored up; will American taxpayers support the rebuilding if they are not? What say will individual property owners have in the face of widespread demolition? And, in the end, will the displaced —not just the evacuees but also the companies and professional firms that already have relocated . . . in Baton Rouge and other Southern cities—even return? Or will they settle down and adapt to new lives?[76]

Workers rushed to repair New Orleans's broken levees in advance of the storms that followed Katrina.

Perhaps the most controversial of all these questions is whether and how New Orleans would rebuild the most storm-vulnerable parts of the city located in low-lying areas, formerly some of the poorest neighborhoods. Most residents of those areas want to rebuild their homes, but city planning experts and others question whether such a plan would be wise. One Louisiana state senator from an east New Orleans district, Ann Duplessis, was told by officials that her poor neighborhoods would never be rebuilt. She said, "My district is gone. It has turned into a wetland, a marsh."[77] Some people proposed changing these vulnerable areas from residential to public use, such as a park or an airport, an idea that drew charges of race discrimina-

tion. Other officials made even more controversial predictions that a rebuilt New Orleans, which before Katrina was home to almost five hundred thousand people, about two-thirds of them black, would be a much smaller city where blacks would be in a minority.

On September 30 Nagin named an advisory commission to report on rebuilding New Orleans, and on October 17 Blanco announced the creation of a corresponding state rebuilding committee. The planning process was expected to be competitive and contentious, with a host of participants advancing their own ideas or protecting their own interests.

Some observers have compared the job of rebuilding New Orleans to the rebuilding

As water from Hurricane Katrina pours over a levee, nearly all of New Orleans is under water.

of Hiroshima, Japan, (nearly leveled in 1945 by the atomic bomb that ended World War II), a process that took some twenty years. But many others, especially business-people, urge the rapid reopening of parts of the city's core that were not significantly destroyed, such as the French Quarter, the Central Business District, and the Garden District, arguing that bringing in vital tourist dollars can sustain New Orleans while the rest of the city is rebuilt. And optimists predict that, eventually, reconstruction can result in an economic rebound for the region. As Judah Hertz, the owner of more than 25 percent of the commercial space in New Orleans's Central Business District, explains, "This has been a terrible tragedy, but it's a chance to arise like a phoenix, to rebuild like never before."[78] The *Times-Picayune* seconded Hertz's vision in a post-Katrina editorial: "The New Orleans that we and the nation deserve will be protected by thriving marshlands, walled off for floods, rebuilt even for its poorest citizens. It will be endowed with the schools, roads and new infrastructure that will allow it once again to be a viable urban center, a vital port, a cultural treasure to America and the world."[79] Similar optimism was expressed by officials in Mississippi and Alabama.

Katrina has come and gone, but most observers agree that its legacy will be felt for decades. Whatever the future of New Orleans, if the nation rises to the challenges ahead, perhaps the storm can one day be viewed as a very painful and expensive wake-up call that spurred the gulf region and the nation to correct past mistakes and prepare for future disasters.

Notes

Introduction: The Worst Disaster in U.S. History

1. Quoted in Fox News, "It Is Not Safe in New Orleans," August 31, 2005. www.foxnews.com/story/0,2933,167 781,00.html.

Chapter 1: In the Path of a Monster

2. Quoted in CBS News, "Katrina Intensifies and Reloads," August 26, 2005. www.cbsnews.com/stories/2005/08/26 /national/main796505_page2.shtml.

3. Quoted in Thomas Hayden, "Storm Experts Feared the Worst," *U.S. News & World Report*, September 17, 2005. www.usnews.com/usnews/news/articles/050917/ 17climate.htm.

4. National Hurricane Center, Hurricane Katrina Advisory Number 23, August 28, 2005. www.nhc.noaa.gov/ archive/2005/pub/al122005.public.023.shtml?.

5. National Weather Service, New Orleans, LA, August 28, 2005, 10:11 AM CDT, NOAA Bulletin. http://wiki source.org/wiki/August_28_2005_10:11_AM_CDT_N OAA_Bulletin.

6. Quoted in *Houston Chronicle,* "New Orleans Mayor Tells Residents to Leave Town," August 30, 2005. www. chron.com/cs/CDA/ssistory.mpl/topstory2/3327126.

7. Quoted in CBS News, "Katrina Makes Landfall," August 30, 2005. www.cbsnews.com/stories/2005/08/27/ national/main798725.shtml.

8. Quoted in Fox News, "Hurricane Katrina Threatens New Orleans," August 28, 2005. www.foxnews.com/story/ 0,2933,167243,00.html.

9. CBS News, "Katrina Strengthens to Category 5," August 28, 2005. www.cbsnews.com/stories/2005/08/28/national/main798788.shtml.

10. Quoted in CVT.ca, "Hundreds Feared Dead from Hurricane in Biloxi," August 31, 2005. www.ctv.ca/servlet/ArticleNews/story/CTVNews/20050830_hurricane_katrina_050829? s_name=&no_ads=.

11. Quoted in Evan Thomas, "The Lost City," *Newsweek*, September 12, 2005. www.msnbc.msn.com/id/9179587/site/newsweek/.

12. Quoted in CBS News, "Katrina Fades, Destruction in Wake," August 29, 2005. www.cbsnews.com/stories/2005/08/29/national/main798862.shtml.

13. Quoted in Hayden, "Storm Experts Feared the Worst."

14. National Hurricane Center, Hurricane Katrina Advisory Number 23.

15. Quoted in MSNBC, "Some Who Stayed Put May Not Live to Regret It," August 30, 2005. www.msnbc.msn.com/id/9117150/.

16. Quoted in Fox News, "It Is Not Safe in New Orleans."

Chapter 2: The Human Tragedy: No Shelter from the Storm

17. Quoted in *USA Today*, "New Orleans Outlook Bleak; 100 Dead in Miss.," August 30, 2005. www.usatoday.com/weather/stormcenter/2005-08-30-katrina_x.htm.

18. Quoted in CNN, "Relief Workers Confront 'Urban Warfare,'" September 1, 2005. www.cnn.com/2005/WEATHER/09/01/katrina.impact/index.html.

19. Quoted in Joyner, "Katrina: People Dying at New Orleans Convention Center," *Outside the Beltway*, September 1, 2005. www.outsidethebeltway.com/archives/11848.

20. Quoted in Adam Nossiter, "New Orleans Mayor Issues 'Desperate SOS,'" Associated Press, September 2, 2005. http://bellaciao.org/en/article.php3?id_article=7979.

21. Julia Reed, "Hope in the Ruins," *Newsweek*, September 12, 2005. www.msnbc.msn.com/id/9190575/site/news week/.

22. Quoted in Helen Kennedy, "Desperate Pleas Surge Across Net," *New York Daily News*, September 2, 2005. www.nydailynews.com/news/story/342698p-292596c. html.

23. Quoted in Kennedy, "Desperate Pleas Surge Across Net."

24. Quoted in Jon Donley, "Nola View: Family Needs Water, Food," August 31, 2005. www.nola.com/weblogs/nola/index.ssf?/mtlogs/nola_nolaview/archives/2005_09 .html#0 75773.

25. Quoted in Jon Donley, "Nola View: Algiers Resident Needs Rescue," September 3, 2005. www.nola.com/weblogs/nola/index.ssf?/mtlogs/nola_nolaview/archives /2005_09.html#0 75773.

26. Quoted in CNN, "Relief Workers Confront 'Urban Warfare.'"

27. Quoted in Millie Ball, "More Survivor Stories," *Times-Picayune*, September 3, 2005.

28. Quoted in Kirk Johnson, "For Storm Survivors, a Mosaic of Impressions," *New York Times*, September 11, 2005.

29. Quoted in Ball, "More Survivor Stories."

30. Quoted in Paul Higgins, "Katrina Victims' Prayer Answered," *Decatur Daily*, September 1, 2005. www.deca turdaily.com/decaturdaily/news/050901/friends.shtml.

31. Quoted in Go New Orleans, "New Orleans for Visitors: Insomnia Notes," September 17, 2005. http://gonew orleans.about.com/.

32. Quoted in Jon Donley, "Nola View: My Sick Grandfather Trapped," September 5, 2005. www.nola.com/web logs/print.ssf?/mtlogs/nola_nolaview/archives/print0770 64.html.

33. Quoted in Barbara Kantrowitz and Karen Breslau,

"Some Are Found, All Are Lost," *Newsweek*, September 19, 2005. www.msnbc.msn.com/id/9287034/.

34. Quoted in Sewell Chan, "Portrait of Mississippi Victims: Safety of Home Was a Mirage," *New York Times*, September 27, 2005.

35. Quoted in Rhoda A. Pickett, "Bay Road Residents Cope with Aftermath," *Mobile Register*, August 31, 2005.

Chapter 3: Responding to the Crisis: Challenge and Controversy

36. Quoted in CNN, "People Making Decisions Hesitated," September 13, 2005. www.cnn.com/2005/US/09/13/kat rina.response/.

37. Quoted in Eric Lipton, Christopher Drew, Scott Shane, and David Rohde, "Breakdowns Marked Path from Hurricane to Anarchy," *New York Times*, September 11, 2005.

38. Quoted in David Gonzalez, "The Victims: From Margins of Society to Center of the Tragedy," *New York Times*, September 2, 2005.

39. Quoted in CNN, "Heroes Make the Best of a Bad Situation," September 8, 2005. www.cnn.com/2005/US/09/08/katrina.heroes/.

40. Larry Bradshaw and Lorrie Beth Slonsky, "The Real Heroes and Sheroes of New Orleans," Socialist Worker Online, September 8, 2005. www.socialistworker.org/20052/556/556_04_RealHeroes.shtml.

41. Quoted in CNN, "Heroes Make the Best of a Bad Situation."

42. Quoted in CNN, "Heroes Make the Best of a Bad Situation."

43. Quoted in Nossiter, "New Orleans Mayor Issues 'Desperate SOS.'"

44. Quoted in Dave Walker, "Robinette Interview with Nagin Was Unforgettable Radio," September 2, 2005. http://robwire.com/?q=node&from=50.

45. Quoted in CBC News Online, "Hurricane Katrina Time-line," September 4, 2005. www.cbc.ca/news/background /katrina/katrina_timeline.html.

46. George Bush, "Bush's Radio Address," *Times-Picayune*, September 3, 2005.

47. Quoted in Gwen Filosa, "Feds Say Crime Wave Is Over," *Times-Picayune*, September 3, 2005.

48. Quoted in Gwen Filosa and Ed Anderson, "Better Days Coming," *Times-Picayune*, September 5, 2005.

49. Quoted in Lisa Rosetta, "Frustrated: Fire Crews to Hand Out Fliers for FEMA," *Salt Lake Tribune*, September 12, 2005. www.sltrib.com/utah.ci_3004197.

50. Quoted in *Meet the Press with Tim Russert*, transcript for September 4, 2005. www.msnbc.msn.com/id/917 9790/.

51. Quoted in Sheryl Gay Stolberg, "La. Senator Returns to Capitol to Denounce Bush," *New York Times*, September 9, 2005.

52. Quoted in *New York Times*, "Ex-Secretary of State Powell Slams Storm Effort," September 9, 2005.

53. Quoted in Lou Dolinar, "Katrina: What Went Right," Real Clear Politics, September 15, 2005. http://realclear politics.com/Commentary/com-9_15_05_LD.html.

Chapter 4: Assessing the Damage

54. Quoted in Blaine Harden and Shankar Vedantam, "Many Displaced by Katrina Turn to Relatives for Shelter," *Washington Post*, September 8, 2005.

55. Quoted in Alex Berenson, "One by One, Reluctant Holdouts Obey Mayor's Order to Leave Their Homes," *New York Times*, September 8, 2005.

56. Quoted in Berenson, "One by One."

57. Quoted in *USA Today*, "Snowball to Reunite with Young La. Owner," September 6, 2005. www.usatoday.com/ printedition/news/20050907/a_katbriefs07.art.htm.

58. Quoted in Reed Johnson and Steven Barrie-Anthony,

"Time Is Running Out for Stranded Pets," *Los Angeles Times*, September 8, 2005.

59. Quoted in Johnson and Barrie-Anthony, "Time Is Running Out for Stranded Pets."

60. Quoted in *New York Times*, "Bush to Survey New Orleans," September 12, 2005.

61. *New York Times*, "Slowly, Pumps Come On to Drain New Orleans," September 12, 2005.

62. Quoted in Dan Barry, "A Black-Green Curtain of Disease and Destruction, Grime and Stench," *New York Times*, September 12, 2005.

63. Quoted in Dina Cappiello, "Report Offers 'Grave' View of Impact on Environment," *Houston Chronicle* September 15, 2005. www.chron.com/cs/CDA/ssistory.mpl/special /05/katrina/3354612.

64. Quoted in Sewell Chan and Andrew C. Revkin, "Water Returned to Lake Contains Toxic Material," *New York Times*, September 7, 2005.

65. Quoted in *New York Times*, "Gulf Fisheries See Slow Recovery," October 1, 2005.

66. Quoted in Jere Longman and Michael Brick, "Water Pours Over Levee, Flooding Dozens of Blocks in New Orleans," *New York Times*, September 23, 2005.

Chapter 5: Moving Forward

67. Quoted in Edmond Andrews, "Budget Office Says Storm Could Cost Economy 400,000 Jobs," *New York Times*, September 7, 2005.

68. Quoted in Steve Holland, "Bush Rules Out Tax Hikes," Reuters, September 16, 2005. http://news.yahoo.com/ s/nm/20050916/pl_nm/katrina_bush_budget_dc.

69. Quoted in Tony Perry, "Debit Card Program Starts, Then Stops," *Los Angeles Times*, September 10, 2005.

70. David Zucchino and Solomon Moore, "Residents Return to Streets of Means," *Los Angeles Times*, September 12, 2005.

71. Quoted in Tony Perry, "Houston Project Draws Out Traumatized Kids," *Los Angeles Times*, September 19, 2005.

72. Quoted in Kantrowitz and Breslau, "Some Are Found, All Are Lost."

73. Quoted in Martha Carr, "City Tries Once Again to Bring Life Back to Shattered Area," *Times-Picayune*, September 27, 2005.

74. Quoted in Nicole Gaouette, "A Hot, Soggy, Grim Homecoming," *Los Angeles Times*, September 28, 2005.

75. James Varney and Jan Moller, "Shortest Cleanup Estimate Is One Year," *Times-Picayune*, September 30, 2005.

76. Peter H. King, "Put to Katrina's Task," *Los Angeles Times*, September 11, 2005.

77. Quoted in King, "Put to Katrina's Task."

78. Quoted in Greg Thomas, "In Battered CBD, Some See Opportunity," *Times-Picayune*, September 12, 2005.

79. *Times-Picayune*, "Our Opinions: Welcome Back, Mr. President," September 12, 2005.

For More Information

Jonathan Alter, "The Other America; An Enduring Shame: Katrina Reminded Us, but the Problem Is Not New," *Newsweek*, September 19, 2005.

Nancy Gibbs, "Act Two: Hurricane Rita Brings a Second Cruel Assault on the Gulf Coast," *Time*, October 3, 2005.

Jeffrey Kluger, "Is Global Warming Fueling Katrina?" *Time Online Edition*, August 29, 2005. www.time.com/time/nation/article/0,8599,1099102,00.html.

Amanda Ripley, "How Did This Happen?" *Time*, September 12, 2005.

Nathan Thornburgh and Plaquemines Parish, "Unsafe Harbor: Natural Barriers That Might Have Slowed Rita and Katrina Were Ruined Long Ago by Human Development Along the Fragile Gulf Coast," *Time*, October 10, 2005.

Alex Tresniowski, "After the Nightmare: Those Who Rode Out the Horror of Hurricane Katrina Share Their Terror and Tears, as a Region Struggles to Cope with the Storm's Hellish Consequences," *People Weekly*, September 12, 2005.

Web Sites

American Red Cross (www.redcross.org). Since its founding in 1881 by American nurse Clara Barton, the American Red Cross has been the nation's premier emergency response organization. Two of the main missions of the American Red Cross are offering neutral humanitarian care to the victims of war and aiding victims of devastating natural disasters.

Federal Emergency Management Agency (www.fema.gov /about/history.shtm). A former independent agency of the federal government that became part of the new Department of Homeland Security in March 2003, FEMA is tasked with responding to, planning for, aiding recovery from, and preventing natural and man-made disasters.

National Hurricane Center (www.nhc.noaa.gov). The National Hurricane Center (NHC) is part of the Tropical Prediction Center, a component of the National Weather Service, a federal agency that provides weather, hydrologic, and climate forecasts and warnings, including detailed, timely satellite imagery and data, for the United States and nearby areas. The NHC maintains a continuous watch for tropical hurricanes during hurricane season and issues forecasts, watches, and warnings that are relied on by U.S. government agencies, foreign governments, the private sector, and the general public to prepare for hurricanes.

NOLA.com (www.nola.com). A Web site affiliated with New Orleans's main newspaper, the *Times-Picayune*, featuring news and information about New Orleans—including daily news stories about the aftermath of Katrina, photos of the city, and a Web log in which storm victims and others tell their stories of evacuation and survival, bravery, fear, and loss.

Index

Picture Credits

About the Author

Debra A. Miller is a writer and lawyer with a passion for current events and history. She began her law career in Washington, D.C., where she worked on legislative, policy, and legal matters in government, public interest, and private law firm positions. She now lives with her husband in Encinitas, California. She has written and edited legal publications, as well as numerous books and anthologies on historical and political topics.